THE GOSPEL OF JESUS CHRIST

FROM BIRTH TO RESURRECTION
WILLIAM THOMAS IRVIN

CONTENTS

PREFACE

THE AIM OF THIS BOOK

There is a record ancient, trustworthy, and profoundly urgent that tells of Jesus Christ. This book invites you to consider that record honestly, whatever doubts you may harbor or questions you may carry. We do not ask you to check your mind at the door. Rather, we ask you to read carefully, to think clearly, and to let the evidence speak for itself.

The Gospel is not complicated, though many have made it so. It is the true account of a life lived, a death suffered, and a resurrection accomplished. It is God's plain answer to humanity's deepest need. This book exists for one simple purpose: to present that Gospel from the Bible, allowing Jesus Christ to speak through His own words and deeds, so that you might understand both who He truly is and what He has done for you.

Why should you read further? Consider this: if God truly loves you, and the Gospel claims that He does, would He leave you ignorant of that love? If you genuinely need salvation, and the Gospel claims that you do, would the God of truth withhold the way to find it? If there exists a Man who claimed to be God's Son, lived a perfect life, died to bear your sins, and rose again from the dead, would that not be the most important fact you could ever know?

This preface makes no elaborate promises. We will not presume to convert you or manipulate your emotions. Only the Holy Spirit of God can do that work. What we offer instead is clarity, the unadorned narrative of Jesus' birth, His earthly ministry, His journey to Jerusalem, His death upon the cross, His burial in the tomb, and His triumph over death in the resurrection. We tell this story not as myth or legend, but as historical reality recorded by those who witnessed it.

You may come to these pages skeptical, indifferent, or even hostile to faith. That concerns us less than the following truth: **you are reading them**. That alone suggests something worthwhile awaits your consideration. The record of Jesus has outlasted empires, survived persecution, and transformed countless lives across centuries. It is not because men were easily fooled, but because Christ's claim upon human hearts is undeniably powerful.

We invite you to meet the Jesus of the Gospels as He actually was, not the sentimental figure of later artistic imagination, nor the political revolutionary some have fashioned, nor the moral teacher others reduce Him to. We invite you to encounter the Christ who spoke as no man ever spoke, who performed miracles that authenticated His deity, who looked upon broken and sinful people with extraordinary compassion, and who deliberately walked toward His own execution because He understood it was the only means by which lost souls could be redeemed.

The Bible records that Christ taught, *"Come unto me, all ye that labour and are heavy laden, and I will give you rest"* (**Matthew 11:28**). This is not the voice of someone seeking to harm you or deceive you. This is an invitation from one who claims to know your condition intimately and to offer you something genuinely valuable, rest for your troubled soul, forgiveness for your sins, and reconciliation with your God.

Throughout these pages, you will encounter the truth that God loves you personally. Not humanity in the abstract, but you, with all your failures, your hidden thoughts, your deepest shame. The Gospel announces that God values you enough to send His own Son, God incarnate, to bear the penalty your sins have earned. This is not duty or obligation speaking. This is love, the deepest, most costly love imaginable.

Yet the Gospel also speaks plainly about your condition. You are a sinner. So are we all. Sin is not reduced to the outrageous crimes that catch the headlines. Sin is turning away from God, the choosing of your own will over His, the transgression of His law, and the corruption this introduces into your very nature. Without Christ, this sin separates you eternally from the God who made you and desires your fellowship. This is not a comfortable truth, but it is an honest one, and honesty, not comfort, is what you need.

Here is where the Gospel becomes good news: Christ died in your place. His death was not tragedy but triumph, the moment God Himself bore the weight of man's sin so that you need not bear it yourself. When Jesus said from the cross, *"It is finished,"* He meant that redemption was complete, that the way had been opened, that **whosoever will** might come to God through faith in Him. Not the worthy, not the successful, not the morally impressive, but whosoever will. That means you.

The Resurrection seals this work. Death could not hold Him because He had conquered sin, death's source and power. His rising proves His claims, validates His sacrifice, and opens a new life to all who trust in Him. The resurrection is not myth or metaphor, it is historical fact witnessed by hundreds and testified to by those who would stake their lives upon it.

This book does not ask you to become religious or to join an institution. It asks you to respond personally to Christ, to acknowledge your sin, to turn from it, and to trust Jesus as your Savior and Lord. This response changes everything. It brings forgiveness, peace, purpose, and the assurance that your eternal destiny is secure in His hands.

Perhaps you have walked from Christ for years. Perhaps you have never truly considered Him. Perhaps you were once close to faith but fell away. Whatever your history, you are welcome here. The Gospel makes no distinction between the outwardly respectable and the openly broken, between the educated and the simple, between those who feel their need and those who think they have none. The invitation is universally extended: **whosoever will may come.**

As you read, we encourage you to read thoughtfully. Consider the evidence. Listen to Christ's own words. Observe His character and His works. Let the scriptures speak for themselves. And as you finish these pages, we hope you will face the central question that the Gospel demands of every soul: What will you do with Jesus Christ?

Your response to that question will determine not only your earthly future, but your eternal destiny. There is no more important decision you could ever make. We pray that as you journey through these pages from the manger to the empty tomb, you will see not only a historical narrative, but the face of the God who loves you and gave Himself for you.

The Gospel awaits your honest consideration. Jesus awaits your personal response. May God grant you eyes to see, ears to hear, and a heart willing to believe.

CHAPTER ONE:
THE PROMISED CHILD

S EVEN CENTURIES BEFORE IT happened, the prophets saw it. In dusty scrolls preserved with trembling reverence, holy men recorded what God Himself had sworn, that into Judah's royal line a Child would come, unlike any child before or since. Isaiah declared, "*Therefore the Lord himself shall give you a sign; Behold, a virgin shall conceive, and bear a son, and shall call his name Immanuel.*" The prophet Micah added with breathtaking precision, "*But thou, Bethlehem Ephratah, though thou be little among the thousands of Judah, yet out of thee shall he come forth unto me that is to be ruler in Israel; whose goings forth have been from of old, from everlasting.*" These were not guesses hurled blindly into the future. They were God's appointed announcements of His own intentions.

Yet who could have imagined that when prophecy met fulfillment, the scene would unfold in such disarming humility? That the virgin would be a young woman of Nazareth, obscure, unheralded, unknown? That the Mighty Ruler would enter the world not in Jerusalem's palace but in Bethlehem's manger? This was no human composition. No earthly author would script the Almighty's entrance in such fashion. It bears every mark of God's authorship, the kind of plan that staggers human wisdom while revealing God's heart.

THE ANGEL'S MESSAGE

Elizabeth, advanced in years and barren, had seemed beyond childbearing, yet God had promised her a son. Now, in her sixth month, Gabriel was sent to a young virgin in Nazareth. He found Mary, a virgin espoused to Joseph, a carpenter descended from King David's royal line. Espousal meant something far more binding than modern engagement; it was a pledge carrying the weight of marriage itself, though the couple did not yet live together. To break such a pledge required formal divorce. Mary stood at that threshold between maidenhood and married life when heaven interrupted her quiet existence.

"Hail, thou that art highly favoured, the Lord is with thee: blessed art thou among women," Gabriel greeted her. Mary was troubled at his saying, turning over in her mind what manner of salutation this could mean. The angel steadied her: *"Fear not, Mary: for thou hast found favour with God. And, behold, thou shalt conceive in thy womb, and bring forth a son, and shalt call his name JESUS. He shall be great, and shall be called the Son of the Highest: and the Lord God shall give unto him the throne of his father David: And he shall reign over the house of Jacob for ever; and of his kingdom there shall be no end."*

Consider what Gabriel announced. This child would be the Son of the Highest, not just a prophet pointing to God, but God's own Son. He would inherit David's throne, fulfilling the ancient covenant God had sworn to David that one of his descendants would reign forever. Yet His kingdom would never end, a detail that could apply to no earthly monarch, for all earthly kingdoms crumble and pass away. The angel was describing deity clothed in humanity, the infinite compressed into the infant. Here was the promise of an eternal kingdom, a reality that transcended human political arrangement entirely.

THE QUESTION AND THE MYSTERY

Mary's response reveals both her faith and her practical wisdom: *"How shall this be, seeing I know not a man?"* She was not doubting God's ability, as Zacharias had done when told his elderly wife would bear a son. Rather, she asked the necessary question, how could a virgin conceive? The very laws of nature denied it. She had not known a man in the intimate sense. She was untouched, pure, a virgin in the fullest meaning of the word.

Gabriel explained the inexplicable: *"The Holy Ghost shall come upon thee, and the power of the Highest shall overshadow thee: therefore also that holy thing which shall be born of thee shall be called the Son of God."* Here was the mechanism, not natural generation, but supernatural creation. The Holy Spirit of God would accomplish what no human agency could perform. The virgin would conceive without a man, carrying within her womb One who was fully human yet fully God.

Why a virgin birth? Because sin passes through the father, transmitted from Adam through every generation of mankind. Had Jesus possessed a human father, He would have inherited Adam's fallen nature, that corruption which courses through the veins of all who descend from Adam. He could not then have been the spotless Lamb, the sinless sacrifice. But conceived by the Holy Spirit in a virgin's womb, Jesus possessed true humanity through Mary while remaining unstained by sin. He could be *"that holy thing,"* set apart, without blemish, the perfect offering God required. This miraculous conception was not God's accommodation to human impossibility; it was His necessary provision. No ordinary birth could produce a sinless Savior.

JOSEPH'S SILENT STRUGGLE

While Mary treasured Gabriel's words in her heart, Joseph faced his own agonizing discovery. The gospel tells us plainly: *"When as his mother Mary was espoused to Joseph, before they came together, she was found with child of the Holy Ghost."* The text does not record who told Joseph or how he learned Mary was pregnant. But learn it he did, and the knowledge must have crushed him. The woman he loved, the woman he was pledged to marry, was carrying a child, and he knew the child was not his.

Joseph was *"a just man,"* the scripture says, and *"not willing to make her a public example."* Justice and mercy warred in his heart. The Law permitted him to divorce her publicly, bringing witnesses to testify against her perceived unfaithfulness. Such a course would have vindicated Joseph but destroyed Mary. Yet instead of claiming his rights, Joseph determined to *"put her away privily,"* to divorce her quietly, minimizing her shame. It was the kindest course available to a man who believed himself betrayed, though it broke his heart to take it.

But God would not leave Joseph to act on incomplete knowledge. *"While he thought on these things, behold, the angel of the Lord appeared unto him in a dream, saying, Joseph, thou son of David, fear not to take unto thee Mary thy wife: for that which is conceived in her is of the Holy Ghost. And she shall bring forth a son, and thou shalt call his name JESUS: for he shall save his people from their sins."*

The angel addressed Joseph as *"son of David,"* reminding him that he stood in the royal line, that through him the legal claim to David's throne would pass to Mary's son. The angel explained what must have seemed impossible: Mary had been faithful. The child within her was not the fruit of sin but the fulfillment of prophecy. What was conceived in her was of the Holy Ghost, divine, miraculous, pure.

And then came the name, pregnant with purpose: *"Thou shalt call his name JESUS: for he shall save his people from their sins."* This child would not come to rescue Israel from Roman oppression, though many would hope for that deliverance. He came to accomplish something far deeper, far more necessary, to save His people from their sins. Not only from sin's consequences, but from sin itself. Not to leave men in their transgressions, but to deliver them out of bondage to iniquity.

Matthew adds a crucial note: *"Now all this was done, that it might be fulfilled which was spoken of the Lord by the prophet, saying, Behold, a virgin shall be with child, and shall bring forth a son, and they shall call his name Emmanuel, which being interpreted is, God with us."* Seven hundred years before, Isaiah had written those words. Now they were fulfilled to the letter, a virgin conceiving, bearing a son, and that son being Emmanuel, *"God with us."* The child in Mary's womb was not only sent from God; He was God stepping into His creation, taking on human flesh to dwell among us.

THE JOURNEY TO BETHLEHEM

Joseph obeyed the angel's command. "*Then Joseph being raised from sleep did as the angel of the Lord had bidden him, and took unto him his wife: and knew her not till she had brought forth her firstborn son: and he called his name JESUS.*" He took Mary as his wife but kept her a virgin until after Jesus was born, preserving the supernatural nature of the conception. Yet they made their home in Nazareth, far from Bethlehem where prophecy demanded the Messiah be born.

God had already set in motion the circumstances that would bring His plan to pass. Far away in Rome, Caesar Augustus, the emperor who ruled the vast Roman Empire, issued a decree "*that all the world should be taxed.*" This was a census, an enrollment requiring every person to register in his ancestral hometown. It was Rome's mechanism for taxation and control. But it was God's instrument to fulfill prophecy.

Joseph "*was of the house and lineage of David,*" and so the decree compelled him to travel to "*the city of David, which is called Bethlehem.*" The journey from Nazareth to Bethlehem stretched some seventy miles, a difficult trek in the best of times, agonizing for a woman in the final days of pregnancy. Yet God's word must be fulfilled. Micah had declared that from Bethlehem would come the Ruler of Israel. And so, though they lived in Nazareth, Joseph and Mary made the arduous journey south to Judea, to the town where David had been born a thousand years before.

BORN IN HUMILITY

"*And so it was, that, while they were there, the days were accomplished that she should be delivered. And she brought forth her firstborn son, and wrapped him in swaddling clothes, and laid him in a manger; because there was no room for them in the inn.*" The simplicity of Luke's narrative cannot obscure the astonishing reality it describes. The Creator of heaven and earth entered His creation in a stable. The King of kings drew His first breath among cattle. The Ruler whose goings forth had been *"from of old, from everlasting"* now lay helpless in a feeding trough, utterly dependent on the virgin mother who had carried Him.

"There was no room for them in the inn." The phrase echoes with heartbreaking irony. The world had no space for its Maker. Bethlehem's crowded lodgings turned away the One who holds all things together. Yet this was not God's miscalculation. This was the plan, that Christ should identify fully with the poor, the displaced, the forgotten. He would know from His first moments what it meant to be unwelcome, to be shut out, to make do with whatever shelter could be found.

The swaddling clothes and manger were not accidents of unfortunate circumstances. They were the appointed markers of the Messiah's arrival. The shepherds would later receive them as a sign: *"Ye shall find the babe wrapped in swaddling clothes, lying in a manger."* What appeared to be the depths of humiliation was actually the depth of God's love, the Almighty stooping to save, the Infinite compressing Himself into infancy, the Holy One lying where animals fed.

GOD'S PLAN REVEALED

Why this child? Why this virgin? Why this stable? The angel had told Joseph the answer: *"He shall save his people from their sins."* Here was the need that drove heaven's plan. Sin had severed man from God. From the moment Adam disobeyed in Eden, every son and daughter born of his line inherited his fallen nature. Sin passed through the generations like a plague, corrupting every human heart. We are born into bondage to sin, slaves of iniquity, unable to free ourselves, doomed to die separated from the God who made us and desires our fellowship.

The Law God gave through Moses revealed the standard of holiness God requires, but it could not impart the power to meet that standard. The sacrifices commanded in the Law, the lambs and bulls offered on

Israel's altars, pointed toward a greater sacrifice to come, but they could never take away sins. Year after year, sacrifice after sacrifice, the offerings were repeated because they could never perfect the worshiper (the one offering them). They were shadows, types, pictures of the true offering God would provide.

And so God made His own provision. He sent His Son, not an angel, not a prophet, but His own beloved Son to do what no human could do. Born of a virgin, Jesus possessed sinless humanity. Conceived by the Holy Spirit, He had no sin to mar His perfection. Living a perfectly obedient life, He fulfilled every requirement of God's righteous Law. And then, for this was the purpose for which He came, He offered Himself as the final, complete sacrifice for sin. Not the blood of animals, but His own precious blood, shed on Calvary's cross to pay the penalty that justice demanded.

"For God so loved the world, that he gave his only begotten Son, that whosoever believeth in him should not perish, but have everlasting life." The manger in Bethlehem was the first step on the road to the cross. The virgin birth made possible the sinless life. The sinless life qualified the perfect sacrifice. And the perfect sacrifice opened the way for sinners, any sinner, every sinner who will come, to be saved from their sins.

This is why Jesus came. Not to establish an earthly kingdom, though He is King. Not to teach moral philosophy, though His words are truth. Not to leave us an example, though His life is the pattern. He came to save. To rescue. To redeem. To pay the price that sinful men and women could never pay. To die the death we deserved so that we might receive the life He earned. To bear the wrath of God against sin so that we might receive the love of God extended to sinners.

The baby in the manger was God's gift to a lost world. *"Unto you is born this day in the city of David a Saviour, which is Christ the Lord."* The prophecies spoken centuries before were fulfilled in every detail, virgin birth, Bethlehem's location, David's lineage. But these facts were not ends in themselves. They were the means to accomplish God's eternal purpose: to provide salvation for whosoever will believe.

As we stand with the shepherds gazing into that manger, we see more than an infant wrapped in swaddling clothes. We see love incarnate. We see hope born into hopelessness. We see God with us, Immanuel, come to seek and to save that which was lost. Every detail of Christ's birth proclaims that God keeps His promises, that His word can be trusted, that His plan of redemption was no afterthought but the eternal purpose of Him who works all things according to the counsel of His own will.

The Promised Child had come, exactly as God had promised. And with His coming, the way of salvation was opened to all who would receive Him.

CHAPTER TWO:
GOD WITH US

T HE INFANT WHO LAY in Bethlehem's manger was destined not to remain hidden in obscurity. But first, the holy Child must be kept safe from the murderous rage of earthly power. God's plan, as always, would not be thwarted by the schemes of men.

THE BIRTH AND TEMPLE PRESENTATION

Jesus was born in Bethlehem, wrapped in swaddling clothes and laid in a manger, fulfilling what the prophets had spoken. On the eighth day, Joseph and Mary brought Him to be circumcised and named Jesus, as the angel had commanded. When the days of Mary's purification were accomplished, they carried Him up to Jerusalem *"to present him to the Lord,"* as it was written in the law. Their offering, *"a pair of turtledoves, or two young pigeons,"* spoke of their humble station, yet God's provision reached every family according to their means.

In the temple that day, two faithful witnesses awaited the Lord's appointment. Simeon, a righteous and devout man upon whom the Holy Spirit rested, had been revealed by the Spirit that he would not see death before beholding the Lord's Christ. Moved by the same Spirit, Simeon came into the temple courts precisely as Mary and Joseph brought Jesus. Taking the Child into his arms, Simeon blessed God and declared with trembling voice: *"Lord, now lettest thou thy servant depart in peace, according to thy word: For mine eyes have seen thy salvation, which thou hast prepared before the face of all people; a light to lighten the Gentiles, and the glory of thy people Israel."* His words proclaimed what the prophets had foreseen, that the Messiah would bring salvation not to Israel alone, but to all peoples.

Anna, a prophetess eighty-four years old, entered at that same instant. She had never left the temple but served God with fastings and prayers night and day. She too gave thanks and spoke of Jesus to all who waited for Jerusalem's redemption. Two witnesses, as the Law required; two voices, as grace had arranged. The truth they testified was sure: this Child was God's promised Redeemer.

Jesus returned with His parents to Nazareth and grew. The scripture declares simply: *"The child grew, and waxed strong in spirit, filled with wisdom: and the grace of God was upon him."*

THE HOUSE IN BETHLEHEM AND THE WISE MEN

After fulfilling the Law in Jerusalem, Joseph and Mary did not immediately return to Nazareth. Instead, they settled in a house at Bethlehem, where they remained for a season. And there, led by a star they understood to herald a King's birth, wise men came from the east seeking Him.

These wise men had first gone to Jerusalem, the natural place to seek a newborn King of the Jews. Their inquiry reached Herod the Great, the Edomite whom Rome had appointed king of Judea. Herod, upon hearing of a rival King, was troubled, and all Jerusalem with him. Herod was a man whose jealous paranoia had driven him to murder members of his own family. The ancient historian Macrobius records that even Caesar Augustus said it was better to be Herod's pig than his son, a dark jest upon a darker truth.

Herod summoned the chief priests and scribes and demanded to know where the Messiah was to be born. They answered from Micah's prophecy: Bethlehem of Judea. Then Herod called the wise men privately, inquired of them the exact time the star appeared, and sent them to Bethlehem with this instruction: *"Go and search diligently for the young child; and when ye have found him, bring me word again, that I may come and worship him also."* It was a lie wrapped in piety. Herod had no intention of worshiping. He intended to murder.

The wise men followed the star until it stood over the place where the young Child was. When they came into the house, they saw Jesus with Mary His mother. They fell down and worshiped Him, opening their treasures and presenting Him gifts: gold, befitting a king; frankincense, used in heaven's worship; and myrrh, the spice of burial. Three gifts. Three truths about the Child they had come to honor, that He would reign, that He was worthy of worship, and that His purpose would require His death.

God warned the wise men in a dream not to return to Herod. They departed into their own country by another way. Their precious gifts, particularly the gold, may have served God's purpose in providing for the family's immediate needs.

FLIGHT INTO EGYPT AND HEROD'S RAGE

After the wise men departed, the angel of the Lord appeared to Joseph in a dream with urgent words: *"Arise, and take the young child and his mother, and flee into Egypt, and be thou there until I bring thee word: for Herod will seek the young child to destroy him."*

Joseph rose immediately. He did not delay to pack carefully or arrange his affairs. By night he took Mary and Jesus and departed for Egypt. They would remain there until Herod's death, a sojourn that fulfilled the word God had spoken through Hosea: *"Out of Egypt have I called my son."* What had been true of Israel as God's collective son in the Exodus was now perfectly fulfilled in Jesus, God's only begotten Son. The nation which Israel had once fled became the refuge of the Messiah.

Back in Bethlehem, Herod's fury erupted when he perceived the wise men had outwitted him. He sent and slew all the male children in Bethlehem and all its borders, from two years old and under, *"according to the time which he had diligently inquired of the wise men."* Jeremiah's ancient lament found its echo: Rachel weeping for her children, refusing to be comforted. Hell's hatred of heaven's King could not have been more starkly displayed. Yet the Child whom Herod sought to destroy was safely beyond his reach, preserved by God's hand in Egypt.

RETURN TO NAZARETH

After Herod died, an angel appeared again to Joseph in a dream: *"Arise, and take the young child and his mother, and go into the land of Israel: for they are dead which sought the young child's life."*

Joseph obeyed and began the journey home. But when he heard that Archelaus, Herod's son, even more brutal than his father, reigned in Judea, Joseph feared to go there. Being warned by God in a dream, Joseph withdrew into Galilee and settled in Nazareth, a village so small and so despised that many would one day ask, *"Can any good thing come out of Nazareth?"* Thus was fulfilled the prophetic word: *"He shall be called a Nazarene."* What appeared to be a detour through geography was actually the unfolding of God's ancient plan, written in the prophets before the world began.

THE HIDDEN YEARS AND GROWTH

For nearly thirty years, the Lord of glory lived in obscurity in Nazareth. A carpenter's son in an obscure town, He waited for the appointed hour when He would begin the work for which He had come. The hands that would one day heal the sick and raise the dead worked wood in a carpenter's shop. He was fully God, yet He submitted to the ordinary rhythms of human childhood and growth, learning, obeying, increasing in wisdom and stature, and in favor with God and man.

THE BOY IN THE TEMPLE

Of those hidden years, scripture gives us one precious glimpse. When Jesus was twelve years old, Joseph and Mary went up to Jerusalem for the

Passover feast, as was their custom. After the feast ended and they began the journey home with their caravan of relatives and friends, Jesus stayed behind in Jerusalem, though His parents did not know it. Assuming He was somewhere among their company, they traveled a full day's journey before they began to search for Him. When they could not find Him, they returned to Jerusalem, seeking Him anxiously.

"And it came to pass, that after three days they found him in the temple, sitting in the midst of the doctors, both hearing them, and asking them questions." Twelve years old, yet His grasp of scripture and His wisdom astonished all who heard Him. When Mary found Him, she said with a mother's reproach mingled with anguish: *"Son, why hast thou thus dealt with us? behold, thy father and I have sought thee sorrowing."*

Jesus answered with words that should have reminded them of His true identity: *"How is it that ye sought me? wist ye not that I must be about my Father's business?"* The temple was His Father's house, and He was there about His Father's business, the work of redemption that would require His blood. At twelve years old, Jesus knew His identity and His purpose with clarity. Yet *"they understood not the saying which he spake unto them."* Even Mary, who had pondered all these things in her heart since the angel's visitation, did not fully grasp what it meant that her Son was the Son of God, that the Child she had nursed and nurtured was God manifest in the flesh.

Jesus returned with them to Nazareth and was subject to them. For eighteen more years He would labor in obscurity, growing *"in wisdom and stature, and in favor with God and man."* Fully human, He experienced the ordinary life of a Jewish man in Nazareth, the work, the fatigue, the hunger, the relationships of a small village. Fully divine, He never once sinned. The sinless life He lived would qualify Him to be the spotless sacrifice. The human life He lived would enable Him to be touched with the feeling of our infirmities, tempted in all points as we are, yet without sin.

THE FORERUNNER APPEARS

When Jesus was about thirty years old, John the Baptist appeared in the wilderness of Judea, preaching repentance and baptizing in the Jordan River. John was the forerunner, the voice crying in the wilderness, *"Prepare ye the way of the Lord, make his paths straight."* He had come to make ready a people prepared for the Lord, baptizing with water unto repentance. But John knew his baptism was incomplete, pointing forward to something infinitely greater. *"I indeed baptize you with water unto repentance,"* he declared, *"but he that cometh after me is mightier than I, whose shoes I am not worthy to bear: he shall baptize you with the Holy Ghost, and with fire."*

THE BAPTISM

Then came Jesus from Galilee to Jordan unto John to be baptized. John tried to prevent Him, saying, *"I have need to be baptized of thee, and comest thou to me?"* John recognized that Jesus, being sinless, had no need of a baptism of repentance. But Jesus answered, *"Suffer it to be so now: for thus it becometh us to fulfil all righteousness."*

When Jesus came up out of the water, something unprecedented occurred. The heavens were opened unto Him, and He saw the Spirit of God descending like a dove, lighting upon Him. A voice from heaven proclaimed: *"This is my beloved Son, in whom I am well pleased."* Here was the attestation, the Father's voice from heaven, the Spirit descending as a dove, and the Son standing in the waters of Jordan. The triune God revealed in one glorious moment, confirming Jesus' identity and mission to all who would believe.

John bore record: *"And I knew him not: but he that sent me to baptize with water, the same said unto me, Upon whom thou shalt see the Spirit descending, and remaining on him, the same is he which baptizeth with the Holy Ghost. And I saw, and bare record that this is the Son of God."*

The next day, John saw Jesus coming toward him and declared with prophetic clarity: *"Behold the Lamb of God, which taketh away the sin of the world."* Here was the central truth of the gospel compressed into one sentence. Jesus is the Lamb, the final, perfect sacrifice to which every Old Testament sacrifice had pointed. He is God's Lamb, provided by God Himself, not by man. And He takes away the sin of the world, not covering it temporarily as the animal sacrifices did, but removing it completely, bearing it upon Himself, carrying it away forever. This was the work He came to do.

TEMPTATION IN THE WILDERNESS

Immediately after His baptism, Jesus was led by the Spirit into the wilderness to be tempted by the devil. For forty days and forty nights He fasted, and afterward He was hungry. The devil came to Him with three temptations, each designed to entice Him to abandon His purpose or to accomplish it by means other than the Father's plan, to take a shortcut around the cross.

First, the tempter said, *"If thou be the Son of God, command that these stones be made bread."* Jesus had the power to turn stones to bread. But He had come to live by faith, not by presumption. He answered, *"It is written, Man shall not live by bread alone, but by every word that proceedeth out of the mouth of God."* Jesus would trust the Father to sustain Him, not use His own power for His own relief. He would endure the hunger, for He would endure far worse, the hunger and thirst and agony of the cross.

Then the devil took Him to the pinnacle of the temple in Jerusalem and said, *"If thou be the Son of God, cast thyself down: for it is written, He shall give his angels charge concerning thee: and in their hands they shall bear thee up, lest at any time thou dash thy foot against a stone."* The devil can quote scripture, but he twists it to serve his purposes. He was tempting Jesus to perform a spectacular sign, to force God to act, to make His Messiahship known by a public miracle, but in an irreverent fashion. Jesus answered, "*It is written again, Thou shalt not tempt the Lord thy God.*" He would not put the Father to the test by demanding a miraculous rescue.

Finally, the devil took Him to a high mountain and showed Him all the kingdoms of the world and their glory, saying, "*All these things will I give thee, if thou wilt fall down and worship me.*" Here was the ultimate temptation, to gain the kingdoms without the cross, to receive the crown without the suffering, to bypass death and claim dominion through compromise. But Jesus came to purchase redemption with His blood, not to seize power through selling His soul. "*Then saith Jesus unto him, Get thee hence, Satan: for it is written, Thou shalt worship the Lord thy God, and him only shalt thou serve.*" Satan departed, and angels came and ministered to Jesus.

Jesus had faced temptation and emerged victorious, not by using His own power to exempt Himself from human struggle, but by wielding the word of God as His weapon, just as we must do. He conquered as a man filled with the Spirit, setting the pattern for every believer's battle against the enemy. He demonstrated that the way to overcome temptation is not through human strength alone, but through faith in God's word and submission to God's will.

THE MINISTRY BEGINS

After John was cast into prison, Jesus returned to Galilee in the power of the Spirit, and His fame spread throughout all the region. He taught in the synagogues and was glorified by all, until He came to Nazareth, where He had been brought up.

On the Sabbath day, Jesus went into the synagogue, as was His custom, and stood up to read. The scroll of the prophet Isaiah was handed to Him, and He found the place where it was written: "*The Spirit of the Lord is upon me, because he hath anointed me to preach the gospel to the poor; he hath sent me to heal the brokenhearted, to preach deliverance to the captives, and recovering of sight to the blind, to set at liberty them that are bruised, to preach the acceptable year of the Lord."* He closed the book, gave it back to the attendant, and sat down. Every eye in the synagogue was fastened on Him. And He began to say unto them, *"This day is this scripture fulfilled in your ears."*

At first they marveled at the gracious words that proceeded from His mouth. But then they began to reason among themselves, *"Is not this Joseph's son?"* They knew Him as the carpenter's son who had grown up among them. How could He claim to be the fulfillment of Isaiah's prophecy? Their familiarity bred contempt, and unbelief took root in their hearts.

Jesus, knowing their thoughts, said to them, *"Ye will surely say unto me this proverb, Physician, heal thyself: whatsoever we have heard done in Capernaum, do also here in thy country."* They wanted signs and wonders to validate His claims. But Jesus told them plainly, *"No prophet is accepted in his own country."* He reminded them that in Elijah's day, though there were many widows in Israel during a great famine, Elijah was sent to none of them, but only to a widow in Zarephath, a city of Sidon, a Gentile woman. And though there were many lepers in Israel in the time of Elisha the prophet, none of them were cleansed except Naaman the Syrian, a Gentile.

The implication was unmistakable: God would pass over unbelieving Israel and extend grace to believing Gentiles. The truth cut like a knife. *"And all they in the synagogue, when they heard these things, were filled with wrath, and rose up, and thrust him out of the city, and led him unto the brow of the hill whereon their city was built, that they might cast him down headlong."* They would have murdered Him then and there. But *"passing through the midst of them he went his way."* His hour had not yet come. When it did come, He would not escape, but would lay down His life willingly for the sheep.

GRACE PROCLAIMED

From Nazareth Jesus went throughout Galilee, teaching in their synagogues, preaching the gospel of the kingdom, and healing all manner of sickness and disease among the people. His fame spread, and great multitudes followed Him. Seeing the crowds, He went up on a mountain, and when He was seated, His disciples came to Him. And He opened His mouth and taught them with words that would echo through the ages.

"Blessed are the poor in spirit: for theirs is the kingdom of heaven. Blessed are they that mourn: for they shall be comforted. Blessed are the meek: for they shall inherit the earth. Blessed are they which do hunger and thirst after righteousness: for they shall be filled. Blessed are the merciful: for they shall obtain mercy. Blessed are the pure in heart: for they shall see God. Blessed are the peacemakers: for they shall be called the children of God. Blessed are they which are persecuted for righteousness' sake: for theirs is the kingdom of heaven."

These Beatitudes turned worldly wisdom upside down. The world says, *"Blessed are the powerful, the proud, the self-sufficient, the ones who take what they want and answer to no one."* Jesus says, *"Blessed are the poor in spirit,"* those who recognize their spiritual bankruptcy and cast themselves on God's mercy. The kingdom belongs to those who know they have nothing to offer God but their need, and who come to Him as beggars seeking bread.

In the Sermon on the Mount, Jesus revealed the righteousness God requires, a righteousness that goes far deeper than external compliance with rules. *"Ye have heard that it was said by them of old time, Thou shalt not kill; and whosoever shall kill shall be in danger of the judgment: But I say unto you, That whosoever is angry with his brother without a cause shall be in danger of the judgment."* Murder begins in the heart with anger. *"Ye have heard that it was said by them of old time, Thou shalt not commit adultery: But I say unto you, That whosoever looketh on a woman*

to lust after her hath committed adultery with her already in his heart."
Adultery begins in the heart with lustful desire.

Jesus was not lowering God's standard but revealing its true height. The
Pharisees congratulated themselves because they had not murdered or
committed physical adultery. But Jesus exposed the sin lurking in every
human heart, the anger, the lust, the pride, the hypocrisy. *"For I say unto
you, That except your righteousness shall exceed the righteousness of the
scribes and Pharisees, ye shall in no case enter into the kingdom of heav-
en."* The righteousness God requires is not only external but internal, a
transformed heart, a renewed mind, a spirit remade by the grace of God.
And only God can accomplish such a work.

COMPASSION FOR SINNERS

But Jesus did not simply teach a higher standard, He came to provide the
power to meet it. And He demonstrated God's heart toward sinners by
the company He kept and the people He touched. The Pharisees com-
plained, *"This man receiveth sinners, and eateth with them."* They meant
it as an accusation. Jesus received it as a commendation. He had come
precisely for sinners, not for those who thought themselves righteous.
His mission was to seek and to save that which was lost.

One day, four men brought a man sick of the palsy to Jesus on a bed.
The house where Jesus was teaching was so crowded they could not get
in. Undeterred, they went up on the roof, removed the tiles, and lowered
the man down in front of Jesus. *"When Jesus saw their faith, he said unto
the sick of the palsy, Son, thy sins be forgiven thee."*

The scribes immediately thought in their hearts, *"Why doth this man
thus speak blasphemies? who can forgive sins but God only?"* They were
right, only God can forgive sins. What they failed to see was that God
stood before them in human flesh. Jesus, knowing their thoughts, said,
*"Why reason ye these things in your hearts? Whether is it easier to say to
the sick of the palsy, Thy sins be forgiven thee; or to say, Arise, and take up
thy bed, and walk? But that ye may know that the Son of man hath power*

on earth to forgive sins, (he saith to the sick of the palsy,) I say unto thee, Arise, and take up thy bed, and go thy way into thine house." Immediately the man arose, took up his bed, and went out before them all, glorifying God.

Notice that Jesus addressed the man's greatest need first, not his physical illness, but his sin. His friends brought him for physical healing. Jesus gave him spiritual healing, and then demonstrated His authority to forgive by healing the body as well. Both healings testified to His deity. Only God can forgive sins, and only God can speak a word and make a man sick of the palsy to walk. The sign authenticated the claim.

One night, a ruler of the Jews named Nicodemus came to Jesus. He came by night, perhaps to avoid being seen, perhaps because he wanted unhurried conversation away from the crowds. He began respectfully: *"Rabbi, we know that thou art a teacher come from God: for no man can do these miracles that thou doest, except God be with him."* Nicodemus was right, but he had not gone far enough. Jesus was not only a teacher from God; He was God come to teach.

Jesus answered, *"Verily, verily, I say unto thee, Except a man be born again, he cannot see the kingdom of God."* Nicodemus, confused, asked, *"How can a man be born when he is old? can he enter the second time into his mother's womb, and be born?"* Jesus explained, *"Verily, verily, I say unto thee, Except a man be born of water and of the Spirit, he cannot enter into the kingdom of God. That which is born of the flesh is flesh; and that which is born of the Spirit is spirit."*

Here was the central truth Nicodemus needed to grasp: no amount of religious effort, no accumulation of good works, no careful observance of the Law could gain entrance to God's kingdom. A man must be born again, born from above, born of the Spirit. It is a supernatural work of God, as mysterious and powerful as the wind. And then came the heart of the gospel, as Jesus told Nicodemus how this new birth becomes possible: *"And as Moses lifted up the serpent in the wilderness, even so must the Son of man be lifted up: That whosoever believeth in him should not perish, but have eternal life. For God so loved the world, that he gave his only begotten Son, that whosoever believeth in him should not perish, but have everlasting life."* The new birth comes through faith in the crucified and risen Christ.

On another occasion, Jesus passed through Samaria and came to a well near the city of Sychar. It was about noon, and He sat down at the well, weary from His journey. A Samaritan woman came to draw water, and Jesus said to her, *"Give me to drink."* The woman was astonished. Jews had no dealings with Samaritans, and no respectable rabbi would speak publicly to a woman, especially one with her reputation. But Jesus showed no regard for the social barriers men erect. He saw not a Samaritan or a woman or a sinner, He saw a soul in need of living water.

The conversation that followed revealed both her spiritual thirst and her moral failure. She had been married five times and was currently living with a man who was not her husband. Yet Jesus did not condemn her. Instead, He offered her what she could find nowhere else: *"Whosoever drinketh of this water shall thirst again: But whosoever drinketh of the water that I shall give him shall never thirst; but the water that I shall give him shall be in him a well of water springing up into everlasting life."* When she realized He was a prophet, and then, astonishingly, the Messiah, she left her water pot and ran to the city, saying, *"Come, see a man, which told me all things that ever I did: is not this the Christ?"* Many Samaritans believed on Him because of her testimony, because Jesus had treated a woman with a broken past as worthy of His time, His truth, and His grace.

And then there was Zacchaeus, the chief tax collector in Jericho. Tax collectors were despised as traitors, working for Rome and growing rich by extorting their own people. Zacchaeus was not only a tax collector but the chief among them, and he was very wealthy. When he heard Jesus was passing through Jericho, he wanted to see Him. But Zacchaeus was short in stature, and the crowd blocked his view. So he ran ahead and climbed up into a sycamore tree.

When Jesus came to the place, He looked up and said, "*Zacchaeus, make haste, and come down; for to day I must abide at thy house.*" The crowd grumbled, "*He is gone to be guest with a man that is a sinner.*" But Zacchaeus stood and said to the Lord, "*Behold, Lord, the half of my goods I give to the poor; and if I have taken any thing from any man by false accusation, I restore him fourfold.*" True repentance produces fruit. Jesus said, "*This day is salvation come to this house, forsomuch as he also is a son of Abraham. For the Son of man is come to seek and to save that which was lost.*"

GOD WITH US

Jesus' miracles were not only displays of power, they were signs pointing to who He is and why He came. When He fed five thousand men (besides women and children) with five loaves and two fish, He demonstrated that He is the Bread of Life, able to satisfy the deepest hunger of the soul. When He walked on water, defying the laws of nature that bind creation, He showed His authority over creation itself. When He healed the sick, gave sight to the blind, and made the lame walk, He revealed His power over the curse that sin had brought into the world.

But perhaps His most audacious claim came in a simple statement: "*I am the way, the truth, and the life: no man cometh unto the Father, but by me.*" Not a way, but the way. Not a truth, but the truth. Not a life, but the life. Every other religious leader has said, "*Follow my teachings and they will lead you to God.*" Jesus said, "*I am God. Come to me.*"

This was the paradox that confounded His contemporaries and still confounds the world today: how could this man, who was born of a virgin in a stable, who grew up in Nazareth, who worked as a carpenter, who walked the dusty roads of Galilee, who grew hungry and thirsty and tired, how could this man be God?

Because He was both. Fully God and fully man. The virgin birth preserved His deity while granting Him true humanity. He was God with us, Immanuel, not God appearing to be human, but God truly becoming human while remaining fully God. He experienced everything we experience, the weariness of a long journey, the pain of rejection, the sting of betrayal, the weight of temptation, yet without sin. He knows our frame, for He shared it. He is touched with the feeling of our infirmities, for He bore them.

And because He lived among us, touched us, wept with us, ate with us, He demonstrated that God is not distant or indifferent to human suffering. When Jesus wept at Lazarus' tomb, He showed us a God who grieves with those who grieve. When He touched the leper whom everyone else avoided, He showed us a God who does not recoil from the outcast. When He forgave the woman caught in adultery, He showed us a God whose mercy triumphs over judgment.

Every word He spoke, every miracle He performed, every person He touched testified to this truth: God has come near. The kingdom of heaven is at hand. And whosoever will may come to Him and find forgiveness, healing, hope, and life, not someday in some distant heaven, but now, today, in this broken world where He walked as one of us, bearing our sorrows, carrying our griefs, all the while moving steadily toward the moment when He would bear our sins upon the cross.

The Lamb of God, announced at His baptism, was walking among us, extending grace to sinners, calling the lost to come home, and preparing to lay down His life for the sheep He came to save. This is God with us. This is the Gospel. This is why He came.

CHAPTER THREE:
TOWARD THE CROSS

A s Jesus turned His face toward Jerusalem, every step was deliberate, every word prophetic. He knew what awaited Him in that ancient city. He had told His disciples plainly, yet they struggled to understand. The cross cast its shadow ever longer as He drew nearer to fulfilling the purpose for which He had come into the world.

THE SET FACE

"And it came to pass, when the time was come that he should be received up, he stedfastly set his face to go to Jerusalem." The moment had come. Jesus had completed His ministry in Galilee. The disciples had been taught, the crowds had witnessed His miracles and heard His teaching. Now He must go to Jerusalem, to the city that kills prophets, to fulfill what had been written of Him in the Law and the Prophets.

This was no accidental trajectory, no circumstance of chance. Luke emphasizes the deliberateness of Jesus' decision by the image of His *"set face"* like flint, unmovable, determined. Though He faced rejection from a village of Samaritans who refused to welcome Him, Jesus did not turn back. Though His disciples did not understand where He was going or why, Jesus pressed forward. His purpose was fixed. His destiny was sealed.

Jesus began to tell His disciples what lay before Him. On the journey, as they went up to Jerusalem, Jesus walked ahead of them, and His disciples were amazed, and those who followed were afraid. Then taking the Twelve again, He began to tell them plainly what was to happen to Him: Saying *"Behold, we go up to Jerusalem; and the Son of man shall be delivered unto the chief priests, and unto the scribes; and they shall condemn him to death, and shall deliver him to the Gentiles: And they shall mock him, and shall scourge him, and shall spit upon him, and shall kill him: and the third day he shall rise again."* This was the third time Jesus had explicitly prophesied His death and resurrection to His disciples.

The disciples had heard these words before, yet they could not grasp them. Their minds refused to accept what their ears heard. When James and John asked if they could sit one on His right hand and one on His left in His glory, they revealed that they still expected Jesus to set up an earthly kingdom, to conquer Rome, to restore Israel to greatness. They had not yet understood that the kingdom Jesus came to establish in His first advent was not of this world, that His throne would be secured not through military victory but through sacrificial death.

Yet Jesus was resolved. Nothing could deter Him. He had set His face toward Jerusalem like a man setting his face toward the place of his execution, walking deliberately to his doom, except that this execution was not a tragedy imposed upon an unwilling victim. It was the very purpose for which He had come. He went willingly, even eagerly, toward the cross. As He would later say in the garden, *"Father, not my will, but thine be done."* He was the Lamb walking willingly to the slaughter, the sacrifice offering Himself freely upon the altar.

THE TRIUMPHAL ENTRY

When Jesus came near to Jerusalem, approaching the city from Bethphage on the Mount of Olives, He sent two disciples ahead, saying to them, *"Go into the village opposite you, and immediately you will find a donkey tied there, and a colt with her. Loose them and bring them to me."* The disciples obeyed, and when anyone asked why they were taking the animals, they answered, *"The Lord hath need of them,"* and the owners let them go.

This was no accident. Jesus was fulfilling a prophecy spoken five hundred years before by Zechariah: *"Rejoice greatly, O daughter of Zion; shout, O daughter of Jerusalem: behold, thy King cometh unto thee: he is just, and having salvation: lowly, and riding upon an ass, and upon a colt the foal of an ass."* The King was coming, not in military conquest, not on a war horse, but riding on a donkey, a symbol of humility and peace. He came not to conquer through force, but to conquer through love and sacrifice.

A very large crowd spread their cloaks on the road as Jesus approached. Others cut branches from the trees and strewed them in the way. The people took palm branches, symbols of national rejoicing, as they had been used to welcome the military hero Simon the Maccabee centuries before. *"And the multitudes that went before him, and that followed, cried, saying, Hosanna to the Son of David: Blessed is he that cometh in the name of the Lord; Hosanna in the highest."*

"Hosanna" means *"save us, we pray."* The people understood that Jesus was the Messiah, the long-awaited King of Israel. But what they meant by Messiah and what Jesus proved to be were two different things. They expected a Messiah who would overthrow Rome, who would restore the kingdom to Israel, who would make them great among nations. They did not understand that Jesus came to conquer sin, not Rome; to establish a spiritual kingdom, not a political one; to make His subjects free indeed, not free from earthly oppressors.

When He entered Jerusalem, *"all the city was moved, saying, Who is this? And the multitude said, This is Jesus the prophet of Nazareth of Galilee."* For a moment, it seemed that Jerusalem might receive her King. The triumphal entry was a public declaration of His Messianic authority.

Yet even as the crowds shouted hosannas, the religious authorities grew more determined to destroy Him. The Pharisees said to one another,

"Perceive ye how ye prevail nothing? behold, the world is gone after him." What they meant was that their authority was being challenged. Jesus was drawing the people's allegiance away from them. And that could not be tolerated.

THE CLEANSING OF THE TEMPLE

Immediately after His triumphal entry, Jesus went to the temple and found it transformed into a marketplace. *"And Jesus went into the temple of God, and cast out all them that sold and bought in the temple, and overthrew the tables of the moneychangers, and the seats of them that sold doves, And said unto them, It is written, My house shall be called the house of prayer; but ye have made it a den of thieves."*

The money changers and the merchants who sold sacrificial animals had taken over the temple court. Pilgrims coming from distant lands needed to exchange their foreign coins for temple currency to pay the temple tax and purchase animals for sacrifice. Instead of serving this genuine religious need, the merchants had made a business of it, gouging the poor and extracting profit from those who had come from afar to worship. The temple, which was meant to be a house of prayer for all nations, had become a den of thieves, a place where greed and exploitation corrupted worship.

Jesus' zeal for the purity of His Father's house burned hot. *"He made a scourge of cords, and cast all out of the temple, both the sheep and the oxen; and poured out the money of the changers, and overthrew the tables."* Can you see it? The money changers scrambling to gather their coins as they scattered across the temple floor, the merchant tables overturned, the animals stampeding. Jesus did not use the whip on the people, but the sight of Him fashioning a whip and His fierce action cleared the temple.

This was an act of authority. The temple had been defiled by those who used its sacred space for personal gain. Jesus, as the One to whom the temple truly belonged, reclaimed it. The temple was restored to its proper purpose, a place where the sick could come and encounter the Lord, where the broken could come and be made whole.

But the chief priests and scribes saw the miracles He performed in the temple, and they heard the children crying out in the temple, *"Hosanna to the son of David!,"* and it displeased them greatly. They asked Jesus, *"Hearest thou what these say?"* Jesus answered, *"Yea; have ye never read, Out of the mouth of babes and sucklings thou hast perfected praise?"* The children understood who Jesus was, even if the religious leaders refused to acknowledge it.

Yet all of this, the triumphal entry, the cleansing of the temple, the open declaration of His Messianic authority, only hardened the resolve of the Sanhedrin to kill Him. They were losing control of the people. Jesus had to be eliminated before His popularity grew any greater. The shadow of the cross grew darker and longer.

JESUS WEEPS OVER JERUSALEM

As Jesus looked out over Jerusalem, the city He had come to save, His heart broke. He saw not just buildings and streets, but a people blind to their own moment of visitation, deaf to the voice of the One who loved them most. *"And when he drew nigh, he saw the city, and wept over it, Saying, If thou hadst known, even thou, at least in this thy day, the things which belong unto thy peace! but now they are hid from thine eyes."*

Jesus was not weeping over His own coming suffering, though He knew what awaited Him in those final hours. He was weeping over theirs, over the destruction that would come upon the city and its people because they had rejected Him. *"For the days shall come upon thee, that thine enemies shall cast a trench about thee, and compass thee round, and keep thee in on every side, And shall lay thee even with the ground, and thy children within thee; and they shall not leave in thee one stone upon another; because thou knewest not the time of thy visitation."*

This prophecy would be fulfilled in devastating detail. In seventy AD, forty years after Jesus spoke these words, the Roman armies would besiege Jerusalem, starving the city into submission, then destroying it utterly. Not one stone would be left standing upon another. The judgment Jesus foresaw would fall upon a people who had rejected Him.

Yet beneath Jesus' warning lay an invitation, an ache of longing: "*O Jerusalem, Jerusalem, thou that killest the prophets, and stonest them which are sent unto thee, how often would I have gathered thy children together, even as a hen gathereth her chickens under her wings, and ye would not!*" How often Jesus had reached out to gather them under His wings, to protect them, to save them. The prophets had come. The apostles would come. The Holy Spirit would come. But they would not come. They refused. They turned away from the only One who could have saved them.

This is the heartbreak of God. Not the cold judgment of a distant deity, but the weeping of a Father over His rebellious children, the tears of a King over a people who would not be saved. Jesus did not come to destroy Jerusalem. He came to save it. But Jerusalem would not have Him. The city that should have received her Messiah would reject Him. And in that rejection lay both their tragedy and, by the grace of God, the salvation of all who would believe.

TEACHING IN JERUSALEM

During His final days in Jerusalem, Jesus taught daily in the temple. His teaching was both invitation and warning, extending grace even as He revealed the deepest hypocrisy of the religious leaders.

The Pharisees and scribes questioned His authority. "*By what authority doest thou these things?*" they demanded. Jesus answered with a counter-question, asking them where John's baptism came from, from heaven or from men. They could not answer, because to acknowledge that John came from God would be to acknowledge that Jesus, whom

John pointed to, was the Messiah. Their silence was the silence of those who know they are defeated but too proud to admit it.

Then Jesus began to speak in parables, confronting the leaders with the reality of their spiritual condition. He told them of a man who planted a vineyard and leased it to husbandmen, then went away. When the time came to gather fruit, he sent his servants to collect his share. But the husbandmen beat some, killed some, and stoned others. Finally, he sent his son, thinking surely they would respect him. *"But when the husbandmen saw the son, they said among themselves, This is the heir; come, let us kill him, and let us seize on his inheritance."* They killed the son and cast him out of the vineyard.

The parable was transparent. The vineyard was Israel. The owner was God. The husbandmen were the religious leaders. The servants sent earlier were the prophets whom Israel had rejected and killed throughout her history. And the son was Jesus Himself. In that moment, the religious leaders heard a picture of their own hearts, their determination to seize power and authority, their refusal to acknowledge God's claim upon them, their willingness to kill the very One sent by God to call them to repentance.

Then Jesus spoke the seven woes upon the scribes and Pharisees, laying bare their hypocrisy for all to see. *"Woe unto you, scribes and Pharisees, hypocrites!,"* this phrase rang out again and again like the tolling of a bell, condemning spiritual blindness and self-righteousness.

The first woe: *"Ye shut up the kingdom of heaven against men: for ye neither go in yourselves, neither suffer ye them that are entering to go in."* The Pharisees, who claimed to be the guardians of God's truth, were actually causing the name of God to be blasphemed. Their rigid legalism, their endless rules and regulations, their focus on external observance while neglecting the heart, all of this became a barrier to genuine faith.

The second woe: *"Ye travel sea and land to make one proselyte; and when he is made, ye make him twofold more the child of hell than yourselves."*

The Pharisees were zealous to convert others to their version of Judaism, but in doing so, they passed on to them not genuine faith but the same spiritual blindness and hypocrisy that enslaved themselves.

The third woe condemned them for focusing on minute details of the Law while neglecting its weightier matters: "*Woe unto you, scribes and Pharisees, hypocrites! for ye pay tithe of mint and anise and cummin, and have omitted the weightier matters of the law, judgment, mercy, and faith: these ought ye to have done, and not to leave the other undone.*" They strained at gnats and swallowed camels, making a great fuss over tiny ceremonial details while committing great injustices, murders, and moral depravities.

The fourth woe: "*Ye blind guides, which strain at a gnat, and swallow a camel. Woe unto you, scribes and Pharisees, hypocrites! for ye make clean the outside of the cup and of the platter, but within they are full of extortion and excess.*" They were like whited tombs, beautiful on the outside, but within full of dead men's bones and all uncleanness. Their external righteousness concealed an interior corruption that was killing their souls.

The fifth woe condemned them for building monuments to the prophets while refusing to hear the prophets' message. "*Ye build the tombs of the prophets, and garnish the sepulchers of the righteous, And say, If we had been in the days of our fathers, we would not have been partakers with them in the blood of the prophets.*" Yet in that very moment, they were about to be partakers with their fathers, they were about to shed the blood of Jesus.

The sixth woe spoke of their spiritual blindness and willful rejection of God's truth. They made converts but could not recognize the Messiah. They studied the scriptures but could not see the One of whom the scriptures spoke.

The seventh woe pronounced upon them the ultimate verdict: "*Ye serpents, ye generation of vipers, how can ye escape the damnation of hell?*"

They were children of their fathers who had killed the prophets, and they were filling up the measure of their fathers. They would be judged for their hypocrisy, their blindness, their refusal to receive the One whom God had sent.

THE HEART OF GOD

Yet even in the midst of these terrible woes, Jesus' heart revealed itself. After pronouncing judgment upon the Pharisees and scribes, He turned His attention to the city itself, and the longing in His words overflowed into anguish: "*O Jerusalem, Jerusalem, thou that killest the prophets, and stonest them which are sent unto thee, how often would I have gathered thy children together, even as a hen gathereth her chickens under her wings, and ye would not!*"

This is the repeated invitation of a rejected lover, the repeated reach of a father toward his wayward children. How often, implying many times, many attempts, many messengers sent by God to call Jerusalem to repentance. Yet each time, Jerusalem had rejected the messengers. Each time, the prophets had been killed, stoned, persecuted. The pattern had repeated century after century. And now, at the climax of history, when God Himself stood before them in the person of His Son, they would reject Him too.

And now, standing at the end of the age, Jesus offered one final invitation, one last chance: "*Come unto me, all ye that are weary and heavy laden, and I will give you rest. Take my yoke upon you, and learn of me; for I am meek and lowly in heart: and ye shall find rest unto your souls. For my yoke is easy, and my burden is light.*" But Jerusalem would not come. The religious leaders would not receive Him. And His last words to the city would be words of abandonment: "*Behold, your house is left unto you desolate. For I say unto you, Ye shall not see me henceforth, till ye shall say, Blessed is he that cometh in the name of the Lord.*"

The King had come riding on a donkey, the symbol of peace and humility. He had cleansed the temple and healed the sick. He had taught the people the kingdom of God and called them to repentance. He had extended grace to sinners and challenged the self-righteous with the depth of God's true demands.

But the city that had been appointed to receive Him would not receive Him. The leaders who should have recognized Him and prepared the way for Him worked instead to destroy Him. The tragedy of it broke God's heart, and yet it was not the end of the story. In that rejection lay the seeds of redemption for all humanity.

And so Jesus set His face toward the cross, toward the hour of darkness and suffering that would soon come, carrying with Him the weight of a rejected love, the sorrow of a people who would not be saved, the knowledge that His blood would be poured out for them whether they received it or not. He knew that by dying, He would make a way for all who would come, not just for the few, but for whosoever would believe.

The journey toward Jerusalem was nearly complete. The triumphal entry had given way to conflict. The joy of being received with hosannas had given way to the weeping over a doomed city. And now Jesus would move toward His final purpose, not to reign as an earthly king, but to lay down His life as the Lamb of God, as the perfect sacrifice for the sins of the world. In His rejection by Israel lay the redemption of all humanity. In His suffering lay our salvation. In His death lay our hope.

CHAPTER FOUR:

THE LAMB SLAIN

T HE HOUR HAD COME. All of history had moved toward this moment, the moment when the Lamb of God would be offered for the sins of the world. What Abraham glimpsed dimly when he raised the knife over Isaac, what Moses established through the Passover lamb in Egypt, what every sacrifice on Israel's altar faintly prefigured, now stood poised to be fulfilled in one final, perfect, complete sacrifice.

THE LAST SUPPER

On the night when He was betrayed, Jesus gathered His twelve disciples in an upper room to celebrate the Passover. For fifteen hundred years, Israel had observed this feast, remembering how God had delivered them from Egypt through the blood of lambs applied to their doorposts. But on this night, Jesus would transform the Passover into something infinitely greater, a memorial of a new covenant to be purchased not with the blood of animals, but with His own precious blood, the only offering that could cleanse the sin of the world.

"And as they were eating, Jesus took bread, and blessed it, and brake it, and gave it to the disciples, and said, Take, eat; this is my body." The bread, broken in His hands, represented His body about to be broken for them, soon to bear the full weight of God's judgment. Then *"he took the cup, and gave thanks, and gave it to them, saying, Drink ye all of it; For this is my blood of the new testament, which is shed for many for the remission of sins."*

Consider the profound reality of what Jesus was pronouncing. The old covenant, established at Sinai through Moses with the blood of animals, could never, not once, not ever, take away sins. Year after year, century after century, the same sacrifices had to be offered again and again because they were fundamentally inadequate, simply masking sin beneath a temporary covering. But Jesus was announcing a new covenant, one that would accomplish what the old could never do: the complete forgiveness and irreversible removal of sins. And this covenant would be ratified not with the blood of bulls and goats, whose blood cried out for more sacrifices, but with His own infinitely precious blood, the blood of God incarnate, whose value transcends all creation.

Jesus added these solemn words, His voice carrying the weight of eternity: *"I tell you I will not drink again of this fruit of the vine until that day when I drink it new with you in my Father's kingdom."* He was looking beyond the cross to the resurrection, beyond the suffering to the glory, beyond the death to the eternal feast in His Father's kingdom. Yet in that moment, every eye fixed upon Him, the cross loomed before Him like an abyss. The Last Supper was both a memorial of His death and an anticipation of His return, yet all hung upon what must come in the hours ahead.

After they had sung a hymn, Jesus and the eleven disciples (Judas had already departed into the night to betray Him) went out to the Mount of Olives. What lay ahead would test every one of them to their very limits. And it would reveal the depths of the Savior's love and the terrible strength of His resolve.

GETHSEMANE

In the garden called Gethsemane on the slopes of the Mount of Olives, Jesus withdrew from the disciples about a stone's throw and knelt down to pray. What happened in that garden reveals both the full humanity and the full deity of Jesus Christ in ways that staggers the

mind and breaks the heart, a mystery so profound that angels drew near
to witness it.

*"Father, if thou be willing, remove this cup from me: nevertheless not
my will, but thine, be done."* Three times Jesus prayed this prayer, each
time with greater intensity, each time as the reality of what awaited
Him pressed down with increasingly crushing weight. And the agony
He experienced was so severe, so overwhelming in its psychological and
spiritual dimensions, that *"his sweat was as it were great drops of blood
falling down to the ground."* Medical science knows this phenomenon,
hematidrosis, where extreme anguish causes blood vessels to rupture
beneath the skin, mingling blood with sweat in a torrent of distress. It
happens only under the most intense psychological and emotional stress,
a condition so rare that physicians have studied it in only a handful of
documented cases. And it seems to have happened to Jesus. The Son of
God, sweating blood in agony.

What was in this cup that Jesus asked the Father to remove? It was not
only the physical suffering of crucifixion, though that would be horror
beyond description, six hours of mounting agony as the body's weight
dragged upon pierced limbs, every nerve screaming. It was not only the
betrayal of Judas, the denials of Peter, or the desertion of all His disciples,
though each of these would pierce His heart with the sting of human
treachery. The cup Jesus faced was something immeasurably deeper and
more terrifying: it was the cup of God's wrath against sin, all the fury of
the Almighty's justice, all the punishment that sin deserves, all the separation from the Father that our rebellion had earned, compressed into
those hours when He would hang upon the cross bearing the cumulative
guilt of every sin ever committed by every sinner who would ever come to
Him. The cup of God's wrath. The cup of abandonment by the Father.
The cup that contained the very definition of hell itself.

Here in Gethsemane, we witness God the Son communing with God
the Father in the darkest hour of all eternity. The question Jesus asked,
silently, urgently, desperately, hung in the night air: *"Is there another way
to redeem the souls of men? Is there any other path to reconciliation?"* The

Father gave no answer. The silence was absolute, unbroken, devastating. It was the silence of godly necessity, the silence that means: There is no other way. No other means of salvation. No other path to reconciliation between holy God and sinful man. No escape. No alternative. No reprieve. The Lamb must be slain. The sacrifice must be made. And Jesus, having submitted fully to the Father's will, not reluctantly, but with determined obedience, accepted the cup. He would drink it to its dregs.

An angel appeared from heaven, strengthening Him for what lay ahead. Jesus rose from prayer, His resolve now unshakable, and found the disciples sleeping from sorrow. *"Why sleep ye?"* He asked them. *"Rise and pray, lest ye enter into temptation."* The hour of darkness was upon them all. And Jesus, having wrestled with the realities ahead and emerged victorious, was ready. Ready to face His accusers. Ready to face the cross. Ready to drink the cup to its bitter end.

THE MACHINERY OF DEATH BEGINS TO TURN

While Jesus was still speaking in the garden, Judas arrived with a great multitude armed with swords and staves, sent by the chief priests and elders, a mob armed for war against one man in prayer. Judas had arranged a signal: *"Whomsoever I shall kiss, that same is he: hold him fast."* The intimate gesture of friendship transformed into the tool of betrayal. He came up to Jesus and said, *"Hail, master,"* and kissed Him. Jesus responded, *"Friend, wherefore art thou come?"* Even in this moment of ultimate treachery, Jesus addressed Judas as friend and gave him one last opportunity to repent. But Judas had made his choice, had crossed a line from which there was no return, and the machinery of death began to turn.

Then they laid hands on Jesus and took Him. Peter, impulsive and fierce, but somewhat clumsy, drew his sword and struck the servant of the high priest, cutting off his ear in a desperate act of defense. But Jesus said, *"Put up thy sword into his place: for all they that take the sword shall perish with the sword. Thinkest thou that I cannot now pray to my Father, and he shall presently give me more than twelve legions of angels?"* Seventy-two thousand angels. One angel had slain one hundred eighty-five thousand Assyrian soldiers in a single night in the Old Testament. Twelve legions of angels could have obliterated the Roman Empire, could have consumed every enemy, could have saved Him from the cross with a word. *"But how then shall the scriptures be fulfilled, that thus it must be?"* Jesus did not come to be delivered from the cross. He came to die upon it. *"The cup which my Father hath given me, shall I not drink it?"* He healed the servant's ear, one final miracle of mercy before His arrest, and then allowed Himself to be bound and led away like a lamb to the slaughter, silent and dignified even as rough hands seized Him.

All the disciples forsook Him and fled, exactly as Jesus had prophesied. They who had sworn they would die with Him could not even stay awake with Him in His hour of need, and now they scattered like sheep when the shepherd was struck. The darkness was complete. Jesus stood alone.

INJUSTICE UPON INJUSTICE

Jesus was led first to Annas, the father-in-law of Caiaphas the high priest, for a preliminary examination. From there He was taken to Caiaphas and the Sanhedrin, the religious leaders of Israel, those who should have known Him, who should have recognized their Messiah. False witnesses were brought in to testify against Him, yet even their lies could not cohere. *"Their witness agreed not together."* The machinery of injustice ground forward anyway. Finally, the high priest put Jesus under oath: *"I adjure thee by the living God, that thou tell us whether thou be the Christ, the Son of God."* Jesus answered with clarity and majesty, *"Thou hast said: nevertheless I say unto you, Hereafter shall ye see the Son of man sitting on the right hand of power, and coming in the clouds of heaven."*

The high priest tore his robes and cried, *"He hath spoken blasphemy; what further need have we of witnesses? behold, now ye have heard his blasphemy. What think ye?"* They answered, *"He is guilty of death."* Then they spat in His face and struck Him with their fists, their eyes blazing with hatred and contempt, saying, *"Prophesy unto us, thou Christ, Who is he that smote thee?"* The religious leaders, who claimed to represent God, mocked and abused the Son of God standing before them. The men who quoted scripture daily now reviled the One of whom scripture spoke. The keepers of the Law now trampled the Author of the Law.

Meanwhile, Peter sat outside in the courtyard, warm and safe by a fire, yet confronted three times by those who recognized him as a disciple of Jesus. Three times Peter denied even knowing Jesus, the last time with cursing and swearing, his voice harsh with false oaths. Immediately the rooster crowed, and Peter remembered the word Jesus had spoken: *"Before the cock crow, thou shalt deny me thrice."* Peter went out and wept bitterly. He had failed his Lord in the darkest hour. The man who declared his willingness to die alongside Jesus now could not even acknowledge knowing Him.

When morning came, the Sanhedrin bound Jesus and led Him to Pontius Pilate, the Roman governor, because they did not have the authority to execute Him. They brought false charges: *"We found this fellow perverting the nation, and forbidding to give tribute to Caesar, saying that he himself is Christ a King."* Pilate questioned Jesus: *"Art thou the King of the Jews?"* Jesus answered, *"Thou sayest."* But when the chief priests accused Him of many things, Jesus answered nothing, so that Pilate marveled greatly. The silence of the Lamb before His shearers fulfilled the ancient prophecy. The silence of innocence standing before human corruption.

Pilate, finding no fault in Jesus, sought to release Him. When he learned that Jesus was from Galilee, he sent Him to Herod Antipas, who had jurisdiction over Galilee and was in Jerusalem for the Passover. Herod was glad to see Jesus, hoping He would perform some miracle for his entertainment, hoping to see a spectacle to amuse himself. But Jesus answered Herod not a word. Herod and his soldiers mocked Him, arrayed Him in a gorgeous robe, and sent Him back to Pilate.

Pilate declared to the chief priests and the people, *"Ye have brought this man unto me, as one that perverteth the people: and, behold, I, having examined him before you, have found no fault in this man touching those things whereof ye accuse him: No, nor yet Herod: for I sent you to him; and, lo, nothing worthy of death is done unto him."* Pilate proposed to chastise Jesus and release Him. But the chief priests and elders stirred up the crowd to demand the release of Barabbas, a murderer and insurrectionist, and to crucify Jesus. They shouted for a murderer to live and the innocent to die.

Pilate's wife sent him a message: *"Have thou nothing to do with that just man: for I have suffered many things this day in a dream because of him."* But Pilate, fearing a riot and wanting to satisfy the crowd, delivered Jesus to be scourged. The Roman soldiers took Jesus, stripped Him naked, and beat Him with a flagellum, a whip embedded with pieces of bone and metal designed to tear the flesh with each stroke. Jesus' back was laid open to the bone, the prophet's words becoming reality: *"The plowers plowed upon my back: they made long their furrows."* Violent stroke after violent stroke, each one tearing deeper into exposed muscle and nerve. Streams of blood poured down His body. When the soldiers grew weary, others took their place, and the scourging continued without mercy, their faces twisted with casual cruelty.

They put a scarlet robe on Him, plaited a crown of thorns and pressed it onto His head, driving the thorns deep into His scalp until blood ran down His face. They put a reed in His right hand and bowed before Him in mockery, saying, *"Hail, King of the Jews!"* They spat on Him and struck Him repeatedly on the head with the reed, driving the thorns deeper into His flesh with each blow. The pain was excruciating, a grinding ache in His skull, blood streaming into His eyes. When the evangelists recorded that His *"visage was so marred more than any man, and his form more than the sons of men,"* they were describing a body so beaten, so mutilated, so disfigured that He was barely recognizable as human.

Pilate brought Jesus out again, saying, *"Behold the man!"* He hoped the crowd would be satisfied with His suffering and release Him. But they cried out, "*Crucify him, crucify him!*" The chief priests declared, "*We have no king but Caesar!*" and threatened Pilate: if he released Jesus, he was no friend of Caesar, no protector of Rome. Pilate, who had found no fault in Jesus, who knew Him to be innocent, who wanted to release Him, finally capitulated to political pressure and the bloodlust of the crowd. He took water and washed his hands before the multitude, saying, "*I am innocent of the blood of this just person: see ye to it.*" A theatrical gesture that changed nothing. The people answered, "*His blood be on us, and on our children.*" After this symbolic agreement to murder, Pilate delivered Jesus to be crucified.

The innocent was condemned. The righteous was treated as the unrighteous. The Son of God was handed over to die by the very people He came to save.

THE CRUCIFIXION

They led Jesus to a place called Golgotha, which means "*the place of a skull,*" a barren, desolate hill reserved for executions. There they crucified Him. Two criminals were crucified with Him, one on His right hand and one on His left, fulfilling the scripture that said He would be "*numbered with the transgressors.*" The righteous One numbered among the wicked, bearing their shame.

Crucifixion was the most cruel and degrading form of execution the Roman Empire had devised, a death sentence designed not simply to kill, but to torture, to degrade, to inflict maximum suffering over an extended period. The victim's hands and feet were nailed to a wooden cross, and he was left to die slowly, over hours or even days, from a combination of shock, dehydration, and asphyxiation. To breathe, the victim had to push himself up on the nails piercing his feet, scraping his torn back against the rough wood, only to collapse again when his strength failed. It was agony designed to last, calculated to prolong suffering. Every breath was purchased with pain. Every moment was torment. Medical historians have documented that crucifixion victims often took hours, sometimes more than a day, to die, hours of mounting agony as the body slowly gave way.

But the physical suffering, horrific as it was, was not the worst of what Jesus endured. Seven hundred years before, the prophet Isaiah had written with startling precision: *"He was wounded for our transgressions, he was bruised for our iniquities: the chastisement of our peace was upon him; and with his stripes we are healed. All we like sheep have gone astray; we have turned every one to his own way; and the LORD hath laid on him the iniquity of us all."*

Jesus was bearing our sins. He who knew no sin became sin for us. The wrath of God that we deserved fell upon Him, not metaphorically, but actually, literally, with terrible reality. The punishment that should have been ours, He took in our place. This was substitution, the innocent dying for the guilty, the righteous suffering for the unrighteous, the Lamb of God offered up to satisfy God's justice so that sinners might be saved. In Gethsemane He had asked if there was another way. There was not. This was the only way. He took the cup.

From the cross, Jesus spoke seven times, and each word was wrung from a body in extremity, purchased with pain beyond measure. The first words He spoke were these: *"Father, forgive them; for they know not what they do."* Even as the soldiers gambled for His garments, particularly a garment without seam woven from the top throughout, even as the crowd mocked Him, shaking their heads and saying, *"If thou be the Son of God, come down from the cross,"* even as the religious leaders sneered at Him, saying, *"He saved others; himself he cannot save,"* Jesus prayed for their forgiveness. This is the heart of God laid bare, not vengeance, not wrath, not the punishment they deserved, but love reaching out even to those who crucified Him.

To one of the criminals crucified beside Him, who turned to Jesus in faith and said, *"Lord, remember me when thou comest into thy kingdom,"* Jesus answered, *"Verily I say unto thee, Today shalt thou be with me in paradise."* Salvation comes not through works or merit, not through years of reformation or moral achievement, but through faith in Jesus Christ. This thief had no time to be baptized, no opportunity to do good works, no chance to live a changed life. But he believed, and Jesus saved him. In that moment of grace extended to the dying thief, we see the gospel in miniature, grace offered to the undeserving, salvation given to the lost, redemption purchased by blood.

From noon until three in the afternoon, darkness covered the land. This was no natural eclipse, the Passover was at full moon, making an eclipse impossible. This was supernatural darkness, a sign of God's judgment falling upon the Son. In that darkness, Jesus bore the full weight of God's wrath against sin. He experienced the separation from the Father that our sins deserved. He tasted the isolation that sin creates, the severance from God that is sin's deepest consequence. The intimate fellowship between Father and Son, a communion unbroken since before time began, was severed. And then He cried out with a loud voice, words that pierce the ages with their anguish: *"My God, my God, why hast thou forsaken me?"* For the first and only time in all eternity, the perfect fellowship between Father and Son was broken. Jesus was forsaken so that we might never be forsaken. He drank the cup of abandonment so that we could know the presence of God.

After this, knowing that all things were now accomplished, the work complete, the debt paid, the sacrifice finished, Jesus said, *"I thirst."* His throat was parched from hours in the Mediterranean sun, His body drained from loss of blood and the trauma of crucifixion. The soldiers filled a sponge with vinegar and put it to His mouth. When Jesus had received the vinegar, He said, *"It is finished."* These words reverberated across heaven and earth with the force of victory. This was not the cry of a defeated victim. It was the shout of a conqueror. Jesus had finished the work the Father gave Him to do. The debt of sin was paid, paid in full, forever, for all who would believe. The sacrifice was complete. The way of salvation was opened. The Lamb had been slain.

Then Jesus cried with a loud voice, *"Father, into thy hands I commend my spirit."* And He bowed His head and gave up His spirit. He did not die because His strength failed, did not expire because His body could no longer endure. He laid down His life willingly, exactly as He had said: "*No man taketh it from me, but I lay it down of myself. I have power to lay it down, and I have power to take it again.*" In that final moment, Jesus exercised the ultimate act of authority, not by survival, but by voluntary submission to death. He chose the moment of His death. He determined the hour.

At the moment of His death, the veil of the temple was torn in two from top to bottom. This veil had separated the Holy of Holies, where God's presence dwelt in unapproachable glory, from the rest of the temple for over a thousand years. Only the high priest could enter, and only once a year with the blood of sacrifice, lest he perish in the presence of God's holiness. But now the veil was torn, and it was torn from top to bottom, not by human hands but by the hand of God Himself. The barrier that had proclaimed judgment for centuries now became the proclamation of mercy, an open gateway inviting sinners, by faith, to draw near. The way into God's presence was opened wide through the blood of Jesus Christ. No more need for priests to mediate between God and man. No more need for animal sacrifices. The final sacrifice had been offered. It was sufficient for all.

The centurion who oversaw the crucifixion, who had witnessed crucifixions before and would witness them again, who had stood by while men died in agony, this hardened Roman soldier witnessed something that day that shook him to his core. When he saw what happened, when he saw how Jesus died, the manner of His death, the dignity with which He faced it, the forgiveness He offered, he glorified God, saying, "*Certainly this was a righteous man.*" Matthew records that he said, "*Truly this was the Son of God.*" Even a pagan Roman soldier recognized that something extraordinary had happened. The One they crucified was no ordinary man.

IT IS FINISHED

"It is finished." Three words in which lies the hope of every sinner who has ever lived or ever will live. The debt is paid. The work is complete. The sacrifice is accepted.

What was finished? The work of redemption. Jesus had accomplished what He came to do, to seek and to save that which was lost, to give His life a ransom for many, to bear the sins of the world, to satisfy the justice of God, to reconcile sinners to their Creator. No more sacrifices are needed. No more blood must be shed. No more atonement can be made, because the atonement is complete and eternal.

Isaiah had prophesied it with stunning precision: *"Yet it pleased the LORD to bruise him; he hath put him to grief: when thou shalt make his soul an offering for sin, he shall see his seed, he shall prolong his days, and the pleasure of the LORD shall prosper in his hand. He shall see of the travail of his soul, and shall be satisfied: by his knowledge shall my righteous servant justify many; for he shall bear their iniquities."*

Every detail had been fulfilled. He was despised and rejected. He was oppressed and afflicted. He was led as a lamb to the slaughter. He was numbered with the transgressors. He made intercession for the transgressors. He poured out His soul unto death. And by His stripes, we are healed.

The significance for every soul is this: every human being who has ever been born or ever will be born stands guilty before a holy God. We have sinned and come short of the glory of God. The wages of sin is death, eternal separation from God, eternal punishment in hell. We cannot save ourselves. No amount of good works, religious observance, or moral improvement can pay the debt we owe. We are utterly bankrupt, spiritually destitute, incapable of redemption by our own efforts.

But God, in His great love, provided what we could not provide for ourselves. *"For God so loved the world, that he gave his only begotten Son, that whosoever believeth in him should not perish, but have everlasting life."* Jesus took our place. He bore our sins. He suffered our punishment. He died our death. And because He did, we can be forgiven, justified, reconciled to God.

When Jesus cried, *"It is finished,"* He was declaring that the way of salvation is complete. There is nothing left for us to do but believe. Not believe *and* be baptized. Not believe *and* keep the Law. Not believe *and* do good works. Simply believe. Trust in Jesus Christ alone for salvation. Receive Him as Lord and Savior. And the moment you do, all your sins, past, present, and future, are forgiven, washed away by the blood of the Lamb. Every accusation is silenced. Every debt is cancelled. Every barrier between you and God is removed.

"There is therefore now no condemnation to them which are in Christ Jesus." No condemnation. Not because we deserve mercy. Not because we've earned forgiveness. Not because our good outweighs our evil. But because Jesus paid it all. The debt is cancelled. The sacrifice is accepted. The Lamb is slain. And whosoever will may come and drink freely of the water of life.

The cross stands at the center of history and at the center of the gospel. It is the place where the love of God and the justice of God meet. It is the place where sin is punished and sinners are pardoned. It is the place where the Lamb of God offered Himself once for all, a perfect sacrifice, sufficient to save all who believe.

And the invitation still stands: *"Come unto me, all ye that labour and are heavy laden, and I will give you rest."* Come to the cross. Come to the Lamb. Come to Jesus. For He alone can save. He alone has paid the price. And in Him alone is there salvation, for *"there is none other name under heaven given among men, whereby we must be saved."*

It is finished. The work is done. The sacrifice is complete. And whosoever will may come.

CHAPTER FIVE:
SEALED IN THE TOMB

T HE STONE WAS ROLLED before the tomb entrance, and with it came a silence heavier than death itself. Jesus Christ, the Lamb of God, lay in a borrowed grave. His ministry had ended. His words were stilled. His hands, which had healed the sick and raised the dead, now lay cold and motionless. To all appearances, it was finished, but not as He had meant it.

THE BURIAL

As evening approached on that dark day, when the sun was beginning to set and the Jewish Sabbath drew near, a man named Joseph of Arimathaea appeared, a man of considerable courage and faith, though his discipleship had been hidden in shadow. Joseph was wealthy and respected, an honourable counsellor who opposed the conspiracy against Jesus and had not consented to the decision to put Him to death.

Breaking with the usual practice, for normally Romans did not permit the burial of crucified criminals, and when they did, executed prisoners were cast into common graves with others, not honored with individual tombs, Joseph went boldly to Pilate and asked for the body of Jesus. Pilate, perhaps relieved that this disturbing business could be concluded, granted the request. Joseph took down the body, his own hands handling with reverence the lifeless form of the One he had come to recognize as Messiah.

And then Nicodemus appeared, the same Nicodemus who had come to Jesus by night in **John 3**, seeking to understand how a man could be born again and receive eternal life. What had happened in the intervening years? Had the conversation about being born again, about receiving eternal life through faith in the Son of Man, finally borne fruit in genuine belief? Whatever his spiritual journey, on this day Nicodemus came forth from the shadows of secrecy to openly honor Jesus in death.

Nicodemus brought with him approximately one hundred pounds of myrrh and aloes, an enormous quantity of spices, enough to properly embalm a body royally, enough to honor a king's burial. Whether this abundance spoke of deep faith and extravagant devotion, or of a last hope held secretly in his heart for resurrection, we cannot say with certainty. But it demonstrated that these two men, Joseph and Nicodemus, counted the cost of their discipleship and paid it willingly.

Together they took Jesus' body, wrapped it carefully in clean linen cloth, and placed the spices among the folds, following the burial customs of their people. Then Joseph laid Jesus in his own new tomb, a cave hewn out of rock, which had never been used before and would never be used again. A tomb belonging to a wealthy man, not to a criminal. A tomb of honor, not of shame.

"And he rolled a great stone to the entrance of the tomb and went away." The stone was sealed. The tomb was closed. Jesus was entombed.

Through all of this, a small band of faithful women watched from a distance, their eyes never leaving Him. *"Mary Magdalene and the other Mary sat opposite the grave,"* their vigil maintained even as Joseph and Nicodemus completed their work and departed. They could not save Him. They could not prevent His death. But they could witness, could watch, could stay faithful. And in staying, they bore witness that this burial was real, this death was certain, and all hope seemed now to be entombed with Him.

PROPHECY FULFILLED IN DETAIL

Seven hundred years before Joseph of Arimathaea was born, the prophet Isaiah had written words that seemed incomprehensibly specific about one who would come: *"And they made his grave with the wicked, and with the rich in his death; although he had done no violence, neither was any deceit in his mouth."*

Think about what Isaiah foretold. The servant of the Lord would be assigned a *"grave with the wicked."* Given the way crucifixion was executed, given that two criminals were crucified on either side of Jesus, given the normal Roman practice of discarding crucified bodies in common graves among the refuse, this prophecy would naturally be fulfilled. Justice would seem to demand that Jesus be buried as a criminal deserves, shamefully, without honor, among the wicked.

Yet Isaiah added another detail: *"and with the rich in his death."* This seemed to contradict the first part of the prophecy. How could the same person be buried both with the wicked and with the rich? Yet that is precisely what happened. Though destined for a criminal's grave, having been crucified among them, Jesus was buried with honor in the tomb of Joseph of Arimathaea, a man of great wealth.

And then Isaiah added the reason this reversal would occur: *"because he had done no violence, neither was any deceit in his mouth."* Jesus was innocent. No violence could be charged against Him, He had never raised a hand in anger, never struck a blow. No deceit had ever passed His lips, He had never spoken a lie, never deceived anyone for selfish gain. His innocence was complete and absolute.

Joseph of Arimathaea, looking upon this righteous man unjustly condemned, could not bear to see Him treated as the wicked deserved. His conscience would not allow the Son of God to be cast into a common grave. So he offered his own new tomb, purchased and prepared for his own burial, and gave it instead to Jesus. In doing so, he fulfilled, unknowingly but perfectly, the prophecy spoken through Isaiah centuries before.

The burial of Jesus demonstrated a truth that runs through all of scripture: God keeps His word. Not one detail of what was written about Messiah fails to come to pass. Every prophecy, every foreshadowing, every type and shadow finds its fulfillment in Jesus Christ. The God who had spoken through the prophets was not a God of vague suggestions, but of precise, detailed, prophetic word that cannot be broken.

THE DISCIPLES' DESCENT INTO DESPAIR

But in the tomb where Jesus lay, the disciples could think only of their devastation. The man they had left everything to follow was dead. The one who had called them, taught them, sent them out to preach and heal, was gone. Everything they had built their lives upon had crumbled.

"We were hoping that he was the one to redeem Israel," two disciples said later that day, walking toward Emmaus with sorrow etched into every word. This phrase, *"we were hoping,"* contains the full measure of their despair. That hope was now dead. Buried in the tomb with Jesus' body.

They had seen Him crucified. They had heard His agonized cry from the cross. They had watched as the centurion thrust a spear into His side and water and blood flowed out. They had witnessed the removal of His body from the cross and its placement in the tomb. Death was real. Final. Irreversible.

Those disciples who had been with Jesus in the upper room, who had taken the Bread and the Cup from His hands only hours before, who had heard Him speak of coming trials and His return, now huddled in fear behind locked doors. The doors were shut. Not only closed, but locked, bolted, fastened, as if barriers and locks could protect them from the same fate that had claimed their Master.

"For fear of the Jews," John tells us, the disciples gathered together in darkness, afraid that the authorities who had executed Jesus would hunt them down next. They had been marked as His followers. They had declared themselves His disciples. And if the religious leaders had executed the Teacher, what would they do to the students?

Peter, who had boasted that he would die with Jesus, found himself hiding, afraid even to acknowledge that he knew Jesus. The denial still burned in his conscience, the cock had crowed, and he had wept bitterly, remembering that he had done the very thing Jesus said he would do. James and John, who had asked to sit on Jesus' right hand and left in His glory, now sat in darkness, wondering if there would be any glory at all.

Thomas, who had always questioned, who had insisted on evidence, was notably absent from their gathering. Whether he had withdrawn in private despair, or whether circumstance had simply separated him from the others, we do not know. But when the disciples later told him, *"We have seen the Lord,"* he would demand the very evidence his temperament craved.

The women, who had been faithful at the cross, who had prepared spices to anoint His body, who had come early to the tomb even on the morning after the Sabbath, these faithful women set out with a practical task but no real hope. They had not come expecting to find a living Jesus. They came to anoint a beloved dead man from Nazareth. Their mission was one of devotion to the memory of One whom they had loved and lost.

Consider what three days of silence meant to those who had believed in Him. Jesus had taught them repeatedly that on the third day He would rise. Yet when the third day came and Jesus apparently remained in the tomb, not one of them seems to have expected the resurrection. The promise had been heard but not believed, overshadowed by the crushing reality of His death.

They had hoped. But hope dies hard when the foundation upon which it rests has been broken. They had believed Jesus was the Messiah. But the Messiah dead in a tomb did not fit their understanding of what the Messiah was meant to be. A dead Messiah was a failed Messiah. A crucified Messiah was a rejected Messiah.

All their hopes had been pinned on a man who lay cold in a borrowed grave. All their future had been dependent on a teacher who would teach no more. All their dreams of being part of the kingdom of God seemed to have died with Him.

THE SILENCE OF SATURDAY

Between the darkness of the cross and the glory of the empty tomb lay a day of profound silence. To understand what occurred during these hours, we must trace the events with care, for the chronology carries deep spiritual significance. Jesus was crucified on Wednesday, the fourteenth of Nisan, Passover itself, and buried that evening before the high Sabbath of the Feast of Unleavened Bread could begin. Thursday, the fifteenth of Nisan, was this sacred high day, when no work could be done and all of Israel rested in obedience to the Law. Friday intervened as an ordinary working day. Then came Saturday, the weekly Sabbath, upon which we now turn our gaze. Yet Saturday itself was not the primary focus of our meditation. Rather, we must look back at the entire three-day period, Thursday through Saturday, during which the Lord's body lay sealed in darkness.

In that tomb, wrapped in burial cloths and entombed in stone, lay the One who had walked the shores of Galilee and touched the sick with healing hands. The form that had climbed mountains and sat by wells, that had embraced children and washed disciples' feet, now lay motionless in silence. For three days and three nights, exactly as He had prophesied, His body remained in the grave. The words He had spoken echoed across those silent hours: "*For as Jonas was three days and three*

nights in the whale's belly; so shall the Son of man be three days and three
nights in the heart of the earth."

Yet more profound than the physical silence of the sealed tomb was
another silence, a silence that seemed to descend upon heaven itself. The
Father who had spoken at His baptism with words of affirmation, *"This*
is my beloved Son, in whom I am well pleased," now remained silent.
The Holy Spirit's power, which had rested upon Jesus throughout His
ministry, seemed withdrawn. The disciples did not understand what was
happening. They could not fathom that they were witnessing, in real
time, the precise fulfillment of their Master's own prophecy. To them,
the silence suggested only one thing: abandonment.

Jesus' followers did not realize that He was not defeated, that He had
not been abandoned, that even in death and in the grave, while His enemies celebrated what they believed was final victory, God was working
according to an eternal plan. But how could they know this? All they
possessed were memories and confusion, fear and the crushing weight
of despair. It seemed as though the story had ended in tragedy.

Some of them must have wrestled with terrible questions. Had they been
deceived? Was Jesus simply another failed messiah, one of several who
had arisen and fallen in recent decades? Had they been duped by miracles that perhaps were coincidence, by teaching that sounded profound
but ultimately proved powerless against the vast machinery of religious
and political authority? The images haunted them: His beaten body
suspended on the cross, blood dripping, thorns tearing His brow, nails
piercing His hands and feet. The mocking faces of the crowd. The casting
of lots for His garments. The unnatural darkness that had covered the
land at noon. His final cry, *"It is finished,"* followed by a silence more
terrible than any scream.

Three days. Three nights. The exact period their Master had prophesied. Yet in their despair, the disciples could not see what those passing
hours were accomplishing. They could not perceive that every moment
drawing them closer to Sunday's dawn was drawing them closer to the

greatest vindication in all of history, the resurrection that would validate every word Jesus had spoken, every claim He had made, every promise He had given.

Throughout it all, there lay the tomb. Sealed with a stone. Guarded. Containing the body of Jesus and, so it seemed, the shattered hopes of all who had believed in Him.

But the silence of Saturday would not endure. The prophecies were not yet finished. The word of God could never be broken. The third day was coming, Sunday, the first day of the week.

The disciples huddled in darkness, unaware that the darkest hour is always the hour before the dawn, not knowing that the silence they mourned was about to be shattered by the greatest miracle ever witnessed. They did not yet understand that death itself was about to be defeated and transformed, that every moment of those three days and three nights had unfolded according to the exact prophecy their Master had given them.

The Lamb had been slain and buried. But the story was not over. Victory was coming.

CHAPTER SIX:

ALIVE FOREVERMORE

T HE DARKEST HOUR HAD passed. Saturday's silence was about to be shattered. The tomb that had swallowed Jesus' body would not keep Him. Death, which had reigned from Adam until this moment, was about to meet its conqueror. The third day had come.

DAWN AT THE EMPTY TOMB

"In the end of the sabbath, as it began to dawn toward the first day of the week, came Mary Magdalene and the other Mary to see the sepulchre." The women who had watched Jesus die, who had seen where He was laid, who had observed the Sabbath in anguished waiting, now came in the early darkness to complete the burial rites they had been unable to finish before sundown on Friday.

They came expecting death. They brought spices to anoint a corpse. Their question as they walked was practical and despondent: *"Who shall roll us away the stone from the door of the sepulchre?"* It was a massive stone, sealed by Roman authority, guarded by Roman soldiers. How could a few ladies move it?

But as they approached, *"behold, there was a great earthquake: for the angel of the Lord descended from heaven, and came and rolled back the stone from the door, and sat upon it."* The earth itself trembled at the resurrection of its Creator. The angel, his countenance like lightning, his raiment white as snow, descended not necessarily to let Jesus out, for

He had already risen and departed, but to let the witnesses in, to make manifest what God had accomplished.

The guards, hardened Roman soldiers trained to fear nothing, *"did shake, and became as dead men."* They who were assigned to guard a dead man found themselves helpless before the living messenger of God. The earth quaked, and the guards quaked.

But when the angel spoke, it was not to the guards. *"And the angel answered and said unto the women, Fear not ye: for I know that ye seek Jesus, which was crucified. He is not here: for he is risen, as he said. Come, see the place where the Lord lay."*

"He is not here." Four words that changed everything. The tomb was empty. Not robbed, the grave clothes lay carefully arranged, exactly as Peter and John would discover moments later. Not desecrated, everything spoke of order, not chaos. Simply empty, because Jesus had risen.

Just *"as he said."* The angel reminded them that Jesus had told them this would happen. He had prophesied His death and resurrection repeatedly. But they had not believed, or could not bring themselves to hope. Now the angel was declaring: everything Jesus said was true. He is alive.

"Come, see the place where the Lord lay." The angel invited them into the tomb to verify for themselves. They were not asked to believe blindly. They were invited to examine the evidence, to look at the empty grave clothes, to see that the body was gone.

Then came the commission: *"And go quickly, and tell his disciples that he is risen from the dead; and, behold, he goeth before you into Galilee; there shall ye see him: lo, I have told you."* The message must be proclaimed. The disciples must be told. Jesus is alive, and they will see Him.

AN ABUNDANCE OF EVIDENCE

The women departed quickly from the tomb *"with fear and great joy; and did run to bring his disciples word."* Fear, not terror, but awe at what they had witnessed. And great joy, for Jesus was alive! The darkness that had oppressed them for three days was shattered. Hope, which had died with Him on the cross, was resurrected.

As they ran, "*behold, Jesus met them, saying, All hail: and they came and held him by the feet, and worshipped him.*" This was not a vision, not a ghost, not a hallucination. They grabbed His feet, physical feet, solid and real. They worshiped Him, not as a dead martyr, but as the living Lord.

Jesus said unto them, "*Be not afraid: go tell my brethren that they go into Galilee, and there shall they see me.*" The first witnesses to the resurrection were women, a fact so startling in first-century culture that no one inventing a story would have included it. In that society, women's testimony was not considered legally valid. Yet God chose women to be the first evangelists of the resurrection.

Mary Magdalene, having reported to Peter and John, returned to the tomb after they left. "*But Mary stood without at the sepulchre weeping: and as she wept, she stooped down, and looked into the sepulchre, and seeth two angels in white sitting, the one at the head, and the other at the feet, where the body of Jesus had lain.*" She did not initially recognize them as angels, grief had clouded her vision.

The angels asked her, "*Woman, why weepest thou?*" She answered, "*Because they have taken away my Lord, and I know not where they have laid him.*" Even standing in the empty tomb, with angels present, Mary could not yet grasp that Jesus had risen. She was looking for a corpse, not a conqueror.

"*And when she had thus said, she turned herself back, and saw Jesus standing, and knew not that it was Jesus.*" He asked her, "*Woman, why weepest thou? whom seekest thou?*" Supposing him to be the gardener, she said, "*Sir, if thou have borne him hence, tell me where thou hast laid him, and I will take him away.*"

Then Jesus spoke one word: "*Mary!*" And immediately she recognized him. "*Rabboni!*" she cried, which is to say, **Master**. His voice broke through her grief. The Good Shepherd called His sheep by name, and she knew Him.

Jesus said unto her, "*Touch me not; for I am not yet ascended to my Father: but go to my brethren, and say unto them, I ascend unto my Father, and your Father; and to my God, and your God.*" Mary went and announced to the disciples, "*I have seen the Lord.*"

But the appearances did not end there. The risen Christ was determined to leave no doubt that He was alive.

That same day, Jesus appeared to Peter, though scripture does not give us the details of this private encounter. One can imagine the grace Jesus extended to the disciple who had denied Him three times.

Later that afternoon, Jesus appeared to two disciples walking to Emmaus, a village about seven miles from Jerusalem. They were discussing everything that had happened, and Jesus himself drew near and walked with them, but "*their eyes were holden that they should not know him.*" He asked them what they were discussing, and they told Him about Jesus of Nazareth, "*which was a prophet mighty in deed and word before God and all the people,*" whom the chief priests and rulers had crucified. "*But we trusted that it had been he which should have redeemed Israel: and beside all this, to day is the third day since these things were done,*" they said, their voices heavy with despair.

Then Jesus, beginning at Moses and all the prophets, expounded unto them in all the scriptures the things concerning himself. When they reached Emmaus and sat to eat, Jesus took bread, blessed it, and brake, and gave to them. "*And their eyes were opened, and they knew him; and he vanished out of their sight.*" Immediately they rose and returned to Jerusalem to tell the eleven.

That same evening, Jesus appeared to the disciples as they were gathered together behind locked doors "*for fear of the Jews.*" Suddenly Jesus stood in the midst of them and said, "*Peace be unto you.*" They were terrified, thinking they had seen a spirit. But Jesus said, "*Why are ye troubled? and why do thoughts arise in your hearts? Behold my hands and my feet, that it is I myself: handle me, and see; for a spirit hath not flesh and bones, as ye see me have."* He showed them His hands and His side, the nail scars and the spear wound. Still they could hardly believe for joy. So Jesus asked, *"Have ye here any meat?"* They gave him a piece of a broiled fish, and of an honeycomb. *"And he took it, and did eat before them."*

This was no ghost, no apparition, no hallucination. Jesus had a physical body, a glorified, resurrection body that could pass through locked doors and vanish at will, yet was solid, tangible, able to eat food. The resurrection was not simply spiritual. Jesus rose bodily from the dead.

Eight days later, Jesus appeared again to the disciples, this time with Thomas present, Thomas who had doubted the testimony of the others, who had said, *"Except I shall see in his hands the print of the nails, and put my finger into the print of the nails, and thrust my hand into his side, I will not believe."* Jesus said to Thomas, *"Reach hither thy finger, and behold my hands; and reach hither thy hand, and thrust it into my side: and be not faithless, but believing."* Thomas answered, *"My Lord and my God!"* Jesus replied, *"Thomas, because thou hast seen me, thou hast believed: blessed are they that have not seen, and yet have believed."*

Later, Jesus appeared to seven disciples by the Sea of Galilee, where He cooked breakfast for them and restored Peter to ministry. He appeared to His half-brother James, who had not believed in Him during His earthly ministry but who became a leader in the Jerusalem church after the resurrection.

And then, as Paul recounts in **1 Corinthians 15**, Jesus *"was seen of above five hundred brethren at once; of whom the greater part remain unto this present, but some are fallen asleep."* Five hundred eyewitnesses! Paul was writing this around fifty-five AD, about twenty-five years after the resurrection, and he was essentially saying, *"If you do not believe me, go ask them yourselves. Most of them are still alive."*

These were not isolated incidents, not momentary visions, not grief-induced hallucinations. Jesus appeared to individuals and to groups, to believers and to skeptics, in Jerusalem and in Galilee, indoors and outdoors, during the day and in the evening, over a period of forty days. He ate with them, talked with them, taught them, allowed them to touch Him. He proved beyond any reasonable doubt that He was alive.

Finally, Jesus appeared to Saul of Tarsus on the road to Damascus. Saul, who had been persecuting the church, who had no reason to invent a resurrection story, was confronted by the risen Christ in a blinding light. *"Saul, Saul, why persecutest thou me?"* Jesus asked. Saul responded, *"Who art thou, Lord?"* And Jesus said, *"I am Jesus whom thou persecutest."* Saul, who became Paul the apostle, spent the rest of his life proclaiming the resurrection of Jesus Christ.

The resurrection is the best-attested fact of ancient history. We have testimony from Matthew, Mark, Luke, and John, all eyewitnesses. We have testimony from Peter, James, and Paul. We have multiple independent accounts that agree on the central facts: the tomb was empty, Jesus appeared to many witnesses, and the disciples were transformed from fearful, doubting men into bold proclaimers of the gospel who were willing to die for their testimony.

These resurrection appearances were not isolated events or pious legends. They were the foundation upon which the entire Christian faith would be built

VICTORY OVER DEATH

The empty tomb changes everything. If Jesus is still dead, then Christianity is a lie, and we are to be pitied above all people. But if Jesus rose from the dead, and the evidence overwhelmingly demonstrates that He did, then every claim He made is validated, every promise He spoke is trustworthy, and the way of salvation He opened is sure.

The resurrection proves that Jesus is who He claimed to be. He said He was the Son of God, and the religious leaders condemned Him for blasphemy. But God the Father vindicated His Son by raising Him from the dead. The resurrection is God's declaration: *"This is my beloved Son. Everything He said is true. Everything He did is approved. His sacrifice for sin is accepted."*

The resurrection proves that Jesus' death accomplished what He said it would. He died for our sins, bearing the full penalty that our rebellion deserved. If He had remained in the tomb, we would have no assurance that His sacrifice was sufficient. But because He rose, we know that the debt is paid, the sacrifice is complete, and God's justice is satisfied.

The resurrection guarantees our forgiveness. *"If Christ be not raised, your faith is vain; ye are yet in your sins."* But Christ **hath** been raised! Therefore, everyone who believeth in Him is forgiven, justified, declared righteous before God. The empty tomb is God's receipt, His stamp of approval on the payment Jesus made.

The resurrection promises our own resurrection. Jesus is *"the firstfruits of them that slept."* His resurrection guarantees ours. Because He lives, we shall live also. Death is not the end for those who belong to Christ. The grave cannot hold us, because it could not hold Him.

The resurrection offers new life now. We are not only saved from hell; we are saved to a new quality of life. *"If ye then be risen with Christ, seek those things which are above, where Christ sitteth on the right hand of God."* The power that raised Jesus from the dead is the same power available to believers today, power to overcome sin, power to live righteously, power to endure suffering, power to witness boldly.

The resurrection gives us hope in the face of death. The sting of death is removed for those who are in Christ. Yes, our bodies will die. Yes, we will be laid in graves. But because Jesus rose, we know that death is not the end. It is a doorway to eternal life with Him.

The resurrection assures us that God keeps His promises. Jesus said He would rise on the third day, and He did. He said He would prepare a place for us, and He has. He said He would come again, and He will. The empty tomb is proof that we can trust every word He has spoken.

The resurrection vindicates those who believe. The world mocked the disciples for following a crucified carpenter. The religious leaders laughed at the idea that this blasphemer could be the Messiah. But God raised Jesus from the dead, and in doing so, God declared that those who believe in Jesus are not fools but wise, not deceived but enlightened, not lost but saved.

"I am he that liveth, and was dead; and, behold, I am alive for evermore, Amen; and have the keys of hell and of death." Jesus holds the keys of death and Hell. He conquered death, and He offers that victory to everyone who believeth.

THE RESURRECTION IS EVERYTHING

The resurrection is the hinge on which all of Christianity turns. Without it, Jesus is just another failed messiah, another good teacher who died a tragic death. With it, Jesus is the Lord of life, the Savior of the world, the hope of humanity. Everything we believe, everything we hope for, everything we stake our lives on rests upon the reality of the empty tomb.

The disciples understood this. They had been hiding behind locked doors in despair. But when Jesus appeared to them, when they saw the risen Christ with their own eyes, they were transformed. They would go on to face persecution, imprisonment, and death. Yet they never wavered in their testimony: Jesus is alive. We have seen Him.

The women understood this. They had come to the tomb expecting to anoint a dead body. Instead, they encountered the living Christ and became the first proclaimers of the resurrection. In a culture that did not value women's testimony, God chose women to bear the first witness to the greatest miracle of all history.

The five hundred witnesses understood this. They risked everything, their reputations, their safety, their very lives, to testify that Jesus had risen from the dead.

And the invitation still stands: *"Believe on the Lord Jesus Christ, and thou shalt be saved."* Believe that He died for your sins. Believe that He rose from the dead. Believe that He is alive forevermore. And you will be saved, not by your works, not by your merit, but by His grace through faith in Him.

The tomb is empty. Jesus is alive. Death is defeated. And whosoever will may come and receive the life He offers, eternal, abundant, glorious life in Him who is the resurrection and the life.

CHAPTER SEVEN:

COME AND SEE

YOU HAVE WALKED WITH us through the pages of this Gospel account. You have seen Jesus born in humility, walked with Him through His ministry of compassion and power, wept with Him on the road to Jerusalem, stood at the foot of His cross, lingered in the darkness of the tomb, and witnessed the glory of His resurrection. You have seen Him for who He truly is: God made manifest in flesh, the Lamb slain for the sins of the world, the conqueror of death and hell.

But now comes the most important question you will ever face: What will you do with Jesus?

GOD'S LOVE

We begin where we must begin, with the heart of God. "*For God so loved the world, that he gave his only begotten Son, that whosoever believeth on him should not perish, but have everlasting life.*"

These words contain within them the sum of all truth about God. God loves. Not coldly, not distantly, not tentatively. God loves the world, this broken, sin-stained world, full of people who have turned from Him, rejected Him, spat upon His name. Yet God loves.

And this love is not passive sentiment. It is active, sacrificial, costly love. God gave His only begotten Son. Not an angel. Not a servant. Not a created being. His own Son, the One who had been with Him from the foundation of the world, the One through whom He made all things. God gave this incomparable treasure for you.

Why? "*That whosoever believeth in him should not perish, but have eternal life.*" God's purpose in sending Jesus, God's passion in redemption, is that you might not perish. That you might have eternal life. That you might know Him and be known by Him forever.

God does not want you to be lost. He does not delight in your destruction. He is not eager to punish you or cast you away. The very opposite is true. God has given everything, His only Son, the price of infinite value, so that you might be saved.

This is the God who made you. This is the God who knows you better than you know yourself, knows every secret thought, every hidden desire, every sin you have never confessed to anyone. And knowing all of this, He loves you still.

MAN'S NEED

Yet we must speak plainly about why your salvation was necessary. We must not soften the truth, for to soften it would be to rob you of hope. The truth is this: "*For all have sinned, and come short of the glory of God.*"

You have sinned. Not once, but many times. Perhaps in your own eyes you count yourself a good person, more righteous than many, living a decent life, hurting few people, doing your duty. But God's standard is not "*better than others.*" God's standard is holiness. God's standard is His own perfect righteousness.

Every moment you live for yourself instead of for God is sin. Every time you choose what you want instead of what He commands is sin. Every unkind word, every lustful thought, every lie, every act of pride, every refusal to forgive, every bit of bitterness harbored in your heart, these are sins. And they matter. They matter to God.

And the scripture warns us: "*The wages of sin is death; but the gift of God is eternal life through Jesus Christ our Lord.*" Death is not only physical death, though that awaits us all. It is eternal separation from

God, judgment, condemnation, an eternity in hell separated from His presence, His love, His mercy. This is not metaphorical language. It is the literal consequence of sin.

You cannot save yourself. You cannot work your way to heaven. You cannot be good enough, righteous enough, or faithful enough to earn God's favor. All your righteousness, all your best efforts, all your self-improvement, it is all, in God's eyes, like *"filthy rags."* You stand before a holy God with no defense, no excuse, deserving only judgment.

Stop here for a moment. Feel the weight of this. You are accountable. Your sins are counted. Your rebellion against your Maker is known. The good you have done does not erase the wrong. The kindness you have shown does not balance the harm. You stand naked before the throne of God, and all your covering falls away.

This is not said to condemn you, but to awaken you. This is not meant to drive you to despair, but to desperation, a desperate hunger for rescue, a longing for a Savior, a reaching out for Someone who can do what you cannot do.

And that Someone has come. He has already done what you cannot do.

THE ONLY WAY TO SALVATION

Jesus Christ died in your place. He bore your sins. He suffered the punishment that you deserved. And He rose from the dead, proving that His sacrifice was sufficient, that God accepted His payment for your sins.

This is the good news, the gospel. Not that Jesus gave us a good example to follow. Not that Jesus taught us how to be better people. Not that Jesus opened a door and left you to walk through it on your own strength. No. Jesus did the work. Jesus paid the price. Jesus purchased your salvation with His own blood.

Think of what this means. You deserved condemnation. Jesus took it. You deserved separation from God. Jesus endured it, hanging on the cross, crying out, "*My God, my God, why hast thou forsaken me?*" He felt the weight of God's judgment so that you would not have to. He took your place. He died your death. He satisfied God's justice and opened the way for His mercy to reach you.

"*That if thou shalt confess with thy mouth the Lord Jesus, and shalt believe in thine heart that God hath raised him from the dead, thou shalt be saved.*"

Notice what salvation requires. Not your goodness. Not your worthiness. Not your achievement. Simply two things: belief and confession.

Belief, not only intellectual agreement that Jesus existed or that He was a good man, but heartfelt trust in Him as your Lord and Savior. It means turning from your sins and placing your complete confidence in Jesus Christ and His work on the cross. It means acknowledging that He is Lord, that He has authority over your life, that His way is right, that His word is true. It means surrendering your life to Him, no longer living for yourself but for Him.

Confession, acknowledging before others that Jesus is your Lord, that you belong to Him, that your allegiance is His. True faith cannot hide. It cannot remain private and secret. It must be confessed, declared, made public. When you come to Christ, you step out of darkness into light. You are no longer ashamed. You are no longer afraid. You openly declare that Jesus is your Savior.

"*For with the heart man believeth unto righteousness; and with the mouth confession is made unto salvation. For the scripture saith, Whosoever believeth on him shall not be ashamed. For there is no difference between the Jew and the Greek: for the same Lord over all is rich unto all that call upon him. For whosoever shall call upon the name of the Lord shall be saved.*"

The promise is open to all. Not to a select few. Not to the righteous or the worthy or the religious. To whosoever will. Jews and Gentiles, rich and poor, educated and simple, moral and immoral, all are invited. You are invited.

There is no other way. Jesus Himself declared, *"I am the way, the truth, and the life: no man cometh unto the Father, but by me."* He is not a way. He is the way. He is not one option among many. He is the only means by which sinners can be reconciled to God. You can believe this or reject it, but you cannot change it. This is the reality upon which the universe stands.

If you are lost, Jesus is the Savior. If you are guilty, Jesus is your Redeemer. If you are dead in sin, Jesus is your resurrection and your life. There is no substitute, no alternative, no other name given among men, whereby we must be saved.

YOUR RESPONSE

What must you do? It is simple, and it is profound.

First, **acknowledge your sin**. Stop pretending that you are good enough. Stop making excuses. Look at yourself as God sees you, as a sinner who has broken His holy law, who deserves His judgment, who stands in need of His mercy. This is not self-condemnation. This is honesty. This is seeing yourself clearly. God already knows the truth about you. The only question is whether you will face it too.

Second, **believe that Jesus Christ is who He claimed to be**, the Son of God, your Savior, your Lord. Believe that His death paid the price for your sins. Believe that His resurrection proved that He is alive and able to save you. Not believe about these facts as though they were simply historical information, but believe in Jesus Christ with all your heart. Let this belief penetrate every part of your being. Trust Him. Place all your hope in Him.

Third, **confess Jesus as your Lord**. Tell Him that from this moment forward, you are surrendering your life to Him. You are no longer trying to run your own life, no longer following your own way. You are placing yourself under His lordship, under His authority, committing yourself to follow Him. This is not easy. This is costly. But this is what it means to be saved.

You need not wait for a better moment. You need not clean yourself up first. You need not understand everything perfectly. None of that is required. Jesus receives sinners. He welcomes the broken, the guilty, the lost. He asks only for your willingness to believe and confess.

If you have never done this, if you have never truly surrendered your life to Jesus Christ, then this is the moment. This very moment, as you read these words, the Spirit of God is speaking to your heart. Do not harden yourself. Do not put it off. Do not tell yourself you will do it later. Later may never come. Later often does not come. How many people have said, *"I will turn to Jesus someday"* and yet that day has never arrived? How many have postponed this decision until death found them unprepared?

You can pray. Right now, you can speak to God. Tell Him you are a sinner. Tell Him you believe Jesus died for your sins and rose from the dead. Tell Him you are turning from your sin and placing your faith in Jesus as your Lord and Savior. Tell Him you want to serve Him for the rest of your life. The words need not be fancy or eloquent. God listens to the sincere cry of a repentant heart. He hears the broken plea. He receives the humble confession.

"Repent therefore, and be converted, that your sins may be blotted out." Repentance means turning around. It means going the opposite direction. It means acknowledging that your way was wrong and committing to follow Christ's way instead. It is not only feeling sorry for your sins, though that may be part of it. It is a genuine turning, a new direction, a new commitment. It is dying to yourself and being born again in Christ.

The moment you believe and confess, you are saved. You are born again. You become a child of God. Your sins are forgiven, not just covered, but forgiven, taken away, cast into the sea of God's forgetfulness. You are justified in God's sight, declared righteous, not because you are righteous, but because Jesus' righteousness is credited to you. Your name is written in the Lamb's Book of Life. You belong to Christ, and nothing, absolutely nothing, can take you from His hand.

FINAL ENCOURAGEMENT

Do you understand the stakes of this moment? You are either walking toward eternal life or toward eternal death. You are either receiving the pardon that Jesus purchased with His blood, or you are rejecting it and facing the consequences of your sin before a holy God. There is no middle ground. There is no neutral position. Every day you do not choose Christ is a day you are choosing against Him.

Every day that you delay is another day you are living in rebellion against the God who made you. Every moment you live outside of Christ is a moment you are separated from the only source of true peace, true joy, true hope, true meaning. You may not feel this separation acutely. The world is skilled at distraction. But it is real. It is present. And it is leading you toward judgment.

And time is short. You do not know when your last day will come. You do not know when God will call your soul from your body. *"Boast not thyself of to morrow; for thou knowest not what a day may bring forth."* A car accident. A sudden illness. A heart that stops beating. None of us are promised tomorrow. The only moment you can be certain of is this one, now.

Jesus is alive. He is seated at the right hand of the Father. He is interceding for sinners who call upon His name. He is holding out His arms to you, inviting you to come. *"Come unto me, all ye that labour and are heavy laden, and I will give you rest. Take my yoke upon you, and learn of me; for I am meek and lowly in heart: and ye shall find rest unto your souls. For my yoke is easy, and my burden is light."*

Do you hear that invitation? It is for you. Jesus is calling to you. He has never stopped calling. He knows your name. He knows your pain. He knows your failures. He knows the emptiness inside you that nothing else can fill. He knows the shame you carry, the regrets that haunt you, the sins that burden your conscience. And knowing all of this, He is saying, Come. Come to me. I will save you. I will forgive you. I will give you peace. I will give you purpose. I will give you eternal life.

What will you do with Jesus? Will you continue to run from Him, to ignore Him, to live as though He does not exist, as though His claims do not matter? Or will you come to Him? Will you acknowledge that you are a sinner in need of a Savior? Will you trust Him with your soul? Will you surrender to Him and follow Him?

The choice is yours. God will not force you. He will not override your free will. But know this: the wages of sin is death, and time is running out. The opportunity to be saved is being offered to you now. Tomorrow is not guaranteed. And eternity is forever.

IF WE CAN HELP

If you have reached this point and you do not know Christ, if you are searching, if you have questions, if you want to know more about what it means to trust Jesus, please know that we are here to help.

If you have made a decision to trust Christ, or if you want to make that decision now, please contact us. We are the people of George County Baptist Church, located at 2126 Hopper Road, Lucedale, Mississippi. We are a family of believers who have found forgiveness, peace, and purpose in Jesus Christ. We have experienced the transformation that comes when a sinner surrenders to the Savior. And we would count it an honor and a joy to help you in your spiritual understanding.

You can visit us on Sunday mornings at 10:30 AM or Sunday evenings at 2:00 PM. You can call us. You can email us. No question is too difficult. No sin is too great. No person is beyond the reach of God's grace. We have been where you are. We understand doubt and fear and the struggle to believe. We have experienced God's mercy, and we want to help you experience it too.

We want to help you understand what it means to trust and serve Jesus. We want to help you find a church home, to connect with other believers, to grow in your faith, to experience the abundant life that Jesus promised. And most importantly, we want to help you know Christ personally, to begin a relationship with the One who loves you more than you can comprehend, who died for you, who rose again for you, who is even now interceding for you before the Father's throne.

The Gospel is real. Jesus is alive forevermore. Salvation is available. The invitation stands open. And it is for you.

"Whosoever will, let him come."